2nd Workshop on Building and Using Comparable Corpora: from Parallel to Non-Parallel Corpora 2009

(BUCC 2009)

AA005189

Held at ACL-IJCNLP 2009

Singapore
6 August 2009

ISBN: 978-1-61738-452-3

Printed from e-media with permission by:

Curran Associates, Inc.
57 Morehouse Lane
Red Hook, NY 12571
www.proceedings.com

Some format issues inherent in the e-media version may also appear in this print version.

Copyright© (2009) by the Association for Computational Linguistics
All rights reserved.

Printed by Curran Associates, Inc. (2010)

For permission requests, please contact the Association for Computational Linguistics
at the address below.

Association for Computational Linguistics
209 N. Eighth Street
Stroudsburg, Pennsylvania 18360

Phone: 1-570-476-8006
Fax: 1-570-476-0860

acl@aclweb.org

Introduction

Research in comparable corpora has been motivated by two main reasons in the language engineering and the linguistics communities. In language engineering, it is chiefly motivated by the need to use comparable corpora as training data for statistical NLP applications such as statistical machine translation or cross-language information retrieval. In linguistics, on the other hand, comparable corpora are of interest themselves in providing intra-linguistic discoveries and comparisons. It is generally accepted in both communities that comparable corpora are documents in one to many languages, that are comparable in content and form in various degrees and dimensions. It was pointed out that parallel corpora are at one end of the spectrum of comparability whereas quasi-comparable corpora are at the other end. We believe that the linguistic definitions and observations in comparable corpora can improve methods to mine such corpora for applications to statistical NLP. As such, it is of great interest to bring together builders and users of such corpora.

Parallel corpora are a key resource as training data for statistical machine translation, and for building or extending bilingual lexicons and terminologies. However, beyond a few language pairs such as English-French or English-Chinese and a few contexts such as parliamentary debates or legal texts, they remain a scarce resource, despite the creation of automated methods to collect parallel corpora from the Web. Interest in non-parallel forms of comparable corpora in language engineering primarily ensued from the scarcity of parallel corpora. This has motivated research into the use of comparable corpora: pairs of monolingual corpora selected according to the same set of criteria, but in different languages or language varieties. Non-parallel yet comparable corpora overcome the two limitations of parallel corpora, since sources for original, monolingual texts are much more abundant than translated texts. However, because of their nature, mining translations in comparable corpora is much more challenging than in parallel corpora. What constitutes a good comparable corpus, for a given task or per se, also requires specific attention: while the definition of a parallel corpus is fairly straightforward, building a non-parallel corpus requires control over the selection of source texts in both languages.

With the advent of online data, the potential for building and exploring comparable corpora is growing exponentially. Comparable documents in languages that are very different from each other pose special challenges as very often, the non-parallel-ness in sentences can result from cultural and political differences.

Following the success of the first workshop on Building and Using Comparable Corpora at LREC 2008 in Marrakech, this second workshop again brings together language engineers as well as linguists interested in the constitution and use of comparable corpora, ranging from parallel to non-parallel corpora. In the larger context of the joint ACL-IJCNLP conference, this time the workshop specifically aimed to solicit contributions from researchers in different geographical regions, in order to highlight in particular the issues with comparable corpora across languages that are very different from each other, such as across Asian and European languages. Research in minority languages is also of particular interest. We are very glad to include papers on languages as varied as Arabic, Chinese, English, French, Japanese, Uyghur and even sign language.

We would like to thank all people who in one way or another helped in making this workshop a success. Our particular thanks go to Ken Church for accepting to give the invited presentation, to the participants of the panel discussion, to the members of the program committee, to the ACL-IJCNLP workshop co-chairs Jimmy Lin and Yuji Matsumoto, and to the members of the local organizing committee. Last but not least we would like to thank our authors and the participants of the workshop.

Pascale Fung, Pierre Zweigenbaum, Reinhard Rapp

Organizers:

Pascale Fung (Hong Kong University of Science & Technology—HKUST)
Pierre Zweigenbaum (LIMSI-CNRS, France)
Reinhard Rapp (University of Mainz, Germany & University of Tarragona, Spain)

Program Committee:

Askar Hamdulla (Xinjiang University, China)
Srinivas Bangalore (AT&T Labs, US)
Lynne Bowker (University of Ottawa, Canada)
Éric Gaussier (Université Joseph Fourier, Grenoble, France)
Gregory Grefenstette (Exalead, Paris, France)
Satoshi Isahara (National Institute of Information and Communications Technology, Japan)
Min-Yen Kan (National University of Singapore)
Adam Kilgarriff (Lexical Computing Ltd, UK)
Philippe Langlais (Université de Montral, Canada)
Rada Mihalcea (University of North Texas, US)
Dragos Stefan Munteanu (Language Weaver, Inc., US)
Grace Ngai (Hong Kong Polytechnic University, Hong Kong)
Carol Peters (ISTI-CNR, Pisa, Italy)
Serge Sharoff (University of Leeds, UK)
Richard Sproat (OGI School of Science & Technology, US)
Mandel Shi (Xiamen University, China)
Yujie Zhang (National Institute of Information and Communications Technology, Japan)

Invited Speaker:

Kenneth Ward Church (Chief Scientist, Human Language Technology Center of Excellence, Johns Hopkins University, US)

Workshop Technical Support:

Ricky Chan Ho Yin (Hong Kong University of Science & Technology)

Table of Contents

Conference Program

Thursday, August 6, 2009

8:45 Welcome and Introduction

Invited Presentation

9:00 *Repetition and Language Models and Comparable Corpora*
Ken Church

10:00 Coffee break

Information Extraction and Summarization

10:30 *Extracting Lay Paraphrases of Specialized Expressions from Monolingual Comparable Medical Corpora*
Louise Deléger and Pierre Zweigenbaum

10:55 *An Extensible Crosslinguistic Readability Framework*
Jesse Kirchner, Justin Nuger and Yi Zhang

11:20 *An Analysis of the Calque Phenomena Based on Comparable Corpora*
Marie Garnier and Patrick Saint-Dizier

11:45 *Active Learning of Extractive Reference Summaries for Lecture Speech Summarization*
Jian Zhang and Pascale Fung

12:10 Lunch break

Thursday, August 6, 2009 (continued)

Statistical Machine Translation

13:50 *Train the Machine with What It Can Learn—Corpus Selection for SMT*
Xiwu Han, Hanzhang Li and Tiejun Zhao

14:15 *Mining Name Translations from Comparable Corpora by Creating Bilingual Information Networks*
Heng Ji

14:40 *Chinese-Uyghur Sentence Alignment: An Approach Based on Anchor Sentences*
Samat Mamitimin and Min Hou

15:05 *Exploiting Comparable Corpora with TER and TERp*
Sadaf Abdul Rauf and Holger Schwenk

15:30 Coffee break

Building Comparable Corpora

16:00 *Compilation of Specialized Comparable Corpora in French and Japanese*
Lorraine Goeuriot, Emmanuel Morin and Béatrice Daille

16:25 *Toward Categorization of Sign Language Corpora*
Jérémie Segouat and Annelies Braffort

16:50 **Panel Session**
Multilingual Information Processing: from Parallel to Comparable Corpora

17:50 End of Workshop

Invited Presentation

Repetition and Language Models and Comparable Corpora

Ken Church
Human Language Technology Center of Excellence
Johns Hopkins University
Kenneth.Church@jhu.edu

I will discuss a couple of non-standard features that I believe could be useful for working with comparable corpora. Dotplots have been used in biology to find interesting DNA sequences. Biology is interested in ordered matches, which show up as (possibly broken) diagonals in dotplots. Information Retrieval is more interested in unordered matches (*e.g.*, cosine similarity), which show up as squares in dotplots. Parallel corpora have both squares and diagonals multiplexed together. The diagonals tell us what is a translation of what, and the squares tell us what is in the same language. I would expect dotplots of comparable corpora would contain lots of diagonals and squares, though the diagonals would be shorter and more subtle in comparable corpora than in parallel corpora.

There is also an opportunity to take advantage of repetition in comparable corpora. Repetition is very common. Standard bag-of-word models in Information Retrieval do not attempt to model discourse structure such as given/new. The first mention in a news article (*e.g.*, "Manuel Noriega, former President of Panama") is different from subsequent mentions (e.g., "Noriega"). Adaptive language models were introduced in Speech Recognition to capture the fact that probabilities change or adapt. After we see the first mention, we should expect a subsequent mention. If the first mention has probability p, then under standard (bag-of-words) independence assumptions, two mentions ought to have probability p^2, but we find the probability is actually closer to $p/2$. Adaptation matters more for meaningful units of text. In Japanese, words (meaningful sequences of characters) are more likely to be repeated than fragments (meaningless sequences of characters from words that happen to be adjacent). In newswire, we find more adaptation for content words (proper nouns, technical terminology and good keywords for information retrieval), and less adaptation for function words, clichés and ordinary first names. There is more to meaning than frequency. Content words are not only low frequency, but likely to be repeated.

Proceedings of the 2nd Workshop on Building and Using Comparable Corpora, ACL-IJCNLP 2009, page 1,
Suntec, Singapore, 6 August 2009. ©2009 ACL and AFNLP

Extracting Lay Paraphrases of Specialized Expressions from Monolingual Comparable Medical Corpora

Louise Deléger
INSERM U872 Eq.20
Paris, F-75006 France
louise.deleger@spim.jussieu.fr

Pierre Zweigenbaum
CNRS, LIMSI
Orsay, F-91403 France
pz@limsi.fr

Abstract

Whereas multilingual comparable corpora have been used to identify translations of words or terms, monolingual corpora can help identify paraphrases. The present work addresses paraphrases found between two different discourse types: specialized and lay texts. We therefore built comparable corpora of specialized and lay texts in order to detect equivalent lay and specialized expressions. We identified two devices used in such paraphrases: nominalizations and neo-classical compounds. The results showed that the paraphrases had a good precision and that nominalizations were indeed relevant in the context of studying the differences between specialized and lay language. Neo-classical compounds were less conclusive. This study also demonstrates that simple paraphrase acquisition methods can also work on texts with a rather small degree of similarity, once similar text segments are detected.

1 Introduction

Comparable corpora refer to collections of texts sharing common characteristics. Very often comparable corpora consist of texts in two (or more) languages that address the same topic without being translations of each other. But this notion also applies to monolingual texts. In a monolingual context, comparable corpora can be texts from different sources (such as articles from various newspapers) or from different genres (such as specialized and lay texts) but dealing with the same general topic. Comparable corpora have been used to perform several Natural Language Processing tasks, such as extraction of word translations (Rapp, 1995; Chiao and Zweigenbaum, 2002) in a multilingual context or acquisition of paraphrases (Barzilay and Lee, 2003; Shinyama and Sekine, 2003) in a monolingual context. In this work[1], we are interested in using comparable corpora to extract paraphrases.

Paraphrases are useful to various applications, including information retrieval (Ibrahim et al., 2003), information extraction (Shinyama and Sekine, 2003), document summarization (Barzilay, 2003) and text simplification (Elhadad and Sutaria, 2007). Several methods have been designed to extract paraphrases, many of them dealing with comparable text corpora. A few paraphrase acquisition approaches used plain monolingual corpora to detect paraphrases, such as (Jacquemin, 1999) who detects term variants or (Pasca and Dienes, 2005) who extract paraphrases from random Web documents. This type of corpus does not insure the actual existence of paraphrases and a majority of methods have relied on corpora with a stronger similarity between the documents, thus likely to provide a greater amount of paraphrases. Some paraphrase approaches used monolingual parallel corpora, *i.e.* different translations or versions of the same texts. For instance (Barzilay and McKeown, 2001) detected paraphrases in a corpus of English translations of literary novels. However such corpora are not easily available and approaches which rely instead on other types of corpora are actively investigated.

Bilingual parallel corpora have been exploited for acquiring paraphrases in English (Bannard and Callison-Burch, 2005) and French (Max, 2008). Comparable corpora are another useful source of paraphrases. In this regard, only closely related corpora have been used, especially and almost exclusively corpora of news sources reporting the

[1] This paper is an extension of the work presented in (Deléger and Zweigenbaum, 2008a) and (Deléger and Zweigenbaum, 2008b), more specifically, a new corpus is added, an additional type of paraphrase (based on neo-classical compounds) is extracted and the evaluation is more relevant.

Proceedings of the 2nd Workshop on Building and Using Comparable Corpora, ACL-IJCNLP 2009, pages 2–10,
Suntec, Singapore, 6 August 2009. ©2009 ACL and AFNLP

same events. (Barzilay and Lee, 2003) generated paraphrase sentences from news articles using finite state automata. (Shinyama and Sekine, 2003) extracted paraphrases through the detection of named entities anchors in a corpus of Japanese news articles. In the medical domain, (Elhadad and Sutaria, 2007) worked with a comparable, almost parallel, corpus of medical scientific articles and their lay versions to extract paraphrases between specialized and lay languages.

We aim at detecting paraphrases in medical corpora in the same line as (Elhadad and Sutaria, 2007) but for French. This type of paraphrases would be a useful resource for text simplification or to help authoring medical documents dedicated to the general public. However, in a French medical context, it is difficult to obtain comparable corpora of documents with a high level of similarity, such as pairs of English scientific articles and their translations in lay language, or news articles reporting the same events used in general language (Barzilay and Lee, 2003; Shinyama and Sekine, 2003). Therefore, in addition to using this type of comparable corpora, we also tried to rely on corpora with less similarity but more easily available documents: lay and specialized documents from various sources dealing with the same overall medical topic.

We describe our experiment in building and exploiting these corpora to find paraphrases between specialized and lay language. Issues at stake involve: (i) how to collect corpora as relevant as possible (Section 2.1); (ii) how to identify passages which potentially convey comparable information (Section 2.2); and (iii) what sorts of paraphrases can be collected between these two types of discourse, which is addressed in Section 2.3, through the identification of two kinds of paraphrases: nominalization paraphrases and paraphrases of neo-classical compounds. An evaluation of the method (Section 2.4) is conducted and results are presented (Section 3) and discussed (Section 4).

2 Material and Methods

2.1 Building comparable corpora of lay and specialized texts

Today, a popular way of acquiring a corpus is collecting it from the Web (Kilgarriff and Grefenstette, 2003), as it provides easy access to an unlimited amount of documents. Here we focus on monolingual comparable corpora of specialized and lay medical French documents, with the objective of identifying correspondences between the two varieties of languages in these documents. We collected three corpora from the Web dealing with the following three topics: nicotine addiction, diabetes and cancer.

When dealing with a Web corpus several issues arise. The first one is the relevance of the documents retrieved to the domain targeted and is highly dependant on the method used to gather the documents. Possible methods include querying a general-purpose search engine (such as Google) with selected key words, querying a domain-specific search engine (in domains where they exist) indexing potentially more relevant and trustworthy documents, or directly downloading documents from known relevant websites. Another important issue specific to our type of corpus is the relevance to the genre targeted, *i.e.* lay vs. specialized. Hence the need to classify each collected document as belonging to one genre or the other. This can be done by automatic categorisation of texts or by direct knowledge of the sources of documents. In order to obtain a corpus as relevant as possible to the domain and to the genres, we used direct knowledge and restricted search for selecting the documents. In the case of the cancer topic, we had knowledge of a website containing comparable lay and specialized documents: the Standards, Options: Recommandations website[2] which gives access to guidelines on cancer for the medical specialists on the one hand and guides for the general public on the same topics on the other hand. This case was immediate: we only had to download the documents from the website. This corpus is therefore constituted of quite similar documents (professional guidelines and their lay versions). The other two corpora (on nicotine addiction and diabetes), however, were built from heterogeneous sources through a restricted search and are less similar. We first queried two health search engines (the health Web portals CISMeF[3] and HON[4]) with key words. Both allow the user to search for documents targeted to a population (*e.g.*, patient-oriented documents). We also queried known relevant websites for documents dealing with our chosen topics. Those were

[2] http://www.sor-cancer.fr/
[3] http://www.cismef.org/
[4] http://www.hon.ch/

French governmental websites, including that of the HAS[5] which issues guidelines for health professionals, and that of the INPES[6] which provides educational material for the general public; as well as health websites dedicated to the general public, including Doctissimo[7], Tabac Info Service[8], Stoptabac[9] and Diabète Québec[10].

The corpus dealing with the topic of diabetes served as our development corpus for the first type of paraphrases we extracted, the other two corpora were used as test corpora.

Once collected, a corpus needs to be cleaned and converted into an appropriate format to allow further processing, *i.e.* extracting the textual content of the documents. HTML documents typically contain irrelevant information such as navigation bars, footers and advertisements—referred to as "boilerplate"—which can generate noise. Boilerplate removal methods can rely on HTML structure, visual features (placement and size of blocks) and plain text features. We used HTML structure (such as meta-information and density of HTML tags) and plain text (such as spotting phone and fax numbers and e-mails, as often appear at the end of documents) to get rid of boilerplate.

2.2 Aligning similar text segments

We hypothesize that paraphrases will be found more reliably in text passages taken from both sides of our comparable corpora which address similar topics. So, as a first step, we tried to relate such passages. We proceeded in three steps:

1. as multiple topics are usually addressed in a single text, we performed topic segmentation on each text using the TextTiling (Hearst, 1997) segmentation tool. A segment may consist of one or several paragraphs;

2. we then tried to identify pairs of text segments addressing similar topics and likely to contain paraphrases. For this we used a common, vector-based measure of text similarity: the cosine similarity measure which we computed for each pair of topic segments in the cross-product of both corpus sides (each segment was represented as a bag of words);

3. we selected the best text segment pairs, that is the pairs with a similarity score equal or superior to 0.33, a threshold we determined based on the results of a preliminary study (Deléger and Zweigenbaum, 2008a).

2.3 Extracting paraphrases

We are looking for paraphrases between two varieties of language (specialized and lay), as opposed to any kind of possible paraphrases. We therefore endeavoured to determine what kind of paraphrases may be relevant in this regard. A common hypothesis (Fang, 2005) is that specialized language uses more nominal constructions where lay language uses more verbs instead. We test this hypothesis and build on it to detect specialized-lay paraphrases around noun-to-verb mappings (a first version of this work was published in (Deléger and Zweigenbaum, 2008b)). A second hypothesis is that medical language contains a fair proportion of words from Latin and Greek origins, which are referred to as neo-classical compounds. The meaning of these words may be quite obscure to non-experts readers. So one would expect to find less of these words in lay texts and instead some sort of paraphrases in common language. We therefore tried to detect these paraphrases as a second type of specialized vs. lay correspondences.

2.3.1 Paraphrases of nominalizations

A first type of paraphrases we tried to extract was paraphrases between nominal constructions in the specialized side (such as *treatment of the disease*) and verbal constructions in the lay side (such as *the disease is treated*). This type of paraphrases involves nominalizations of verbal phrases and is built around the relation between a deverbal noun (*e.g. treatment*) and its base verb (*e.g. treat*). Therefore, we relied on a lexicon of French deverbal nouns paired with corresponding verbs (Hathout et al., 2002) to detect such pairs in the corpus segments. These noun-verb pairs served as anchors for the detection of paraphrases. In order to design paraphrasing patterns we extracted all pairs of deverbal noun and verb with their contexts from the development corpus. The study of such pairs with their contexts allowed us to establish a set of lexico-syntactic paraphrasing patterns[11]. An example of such patterns can be seen in Table 1.

[5] http://www.has-sante.fr/
[6] http://www.inpes.sante.fr/
[7] http://www.doctissimo.fr/
[8] http://www.tabac-info-service.fr/
[9] http://www.stop-tabac.ch/
[10] http://www.diabete.qc.ca/

[11] Texts were first tagged with Treetagger (http://www.ims.uni-stuttgart.de/projekte/corplex/TreeTagger/).

Specialized	Lay
N_1 PREP (DET) N_2	V_1 (DET) N_2
N_1 PREP (DET) N_2A_3	V_1(DET) N_2A_3
N_1 A_2	V_1(DET) N_2

Table 1: Example paraphrasing patterns (a shared index indicates equality or synonymy. N=noun, V=verb, A=adjective, PREP=preposition, DET=determiner, 1 in index = pair of deverbal noun and verb)

The general method was to look for corresponding content words (mainly noun and adjective) in the contexts. We defined corresponding words as either equal or synonymous (we used lexicons of synonyms as resources[12]). Equals may have either the same part-of-speech, or different parts-of-speech, in which case stemming[13] is performed to take care of derivational variation (*e.g.*, *medicine* and *medical*). We then applied the patterns to both development and test corpora.

The patterns thus designed are close to the transformation rules of (Jacquemin, 1999) who detects morpho-syntactico-semantic variants of terms in plain monolingual corpora. One difference is that our patterns are built around one specific type of morphological variation (noun to verb variation) that seemed relevant in the context of the specialized/lay opposition, as opposed to any possible variation. We also identify the paraphrases by comparing the two sides of a comparable corpus while (Jacquemin, 1999) starts from a given list of terms and searches for their variants in a plain monolingual corpus. Finally, we do not apply our method on terms specifically but on any expression corresponding to the patterns.

2.3.2 Paraphrases of neo-classical compounds

We then extracted paraphrases of neo-classical compounds as a second type of paraphrases that seemed relevant to the opposition between lay and specialized languages. This means that we looked for neo-classical compounds on one side of the corpora and equivalents in modern language on the other side. To do this we relied on the morphosemantic parser DériF (Namer and Zweigenbaum, 2004). DériF analyzes morphologically complex words and outputs a decomposition of those words into their components and a definition-like gloss of the words according to the meaning of the components in modern language when they are from Greek or Latin origins. For instance the French word *gastrite* (*gastritis*) is decomposed into *gastr+ite* and its gloss is *inflammation de l'estomac* (*inflammation of stomach*).

We first ran the analyzer on the specialized side of the corpora to detect neo-classical compounds. Then we searched for paraphrases of those compounds based on the output of DériF, that is we looked for the modern-language equivalents of the word components (in the case of *gastritis* this means searching for *inflammation* and *stomach*) close to each other within a syntactic phrase (we empirically set a threshold of 4 words as the maximum distance between the modern-language translations of the components). A pattern used to search those paraphrases is for instance:

$$\text{C} \rightarrow \text{((DET)? N PREP)? (DET)? } C_1 \text{ W}^{0-4} \; C_2$$

where C is a neo-classical compounds in a specialized text segment, C_1 and C_2 are the modern-language components of C, N is a noun, PREP a preposition, DET a determiner and W an arbitrary word.

2.4 Evaluation

We first evaluated the quality of the extracted paraphrases by measuring their precision, that is, the percentage of correct results over the entire results. We computed precision for each type of paraphrases.

We then estimated recall for the first type of paraphrases (nominalization paraphrases): the percentage of correct extracted paraphrases over the total number of paraphrases that should have been extracted. We used as gold standard a random sample of 10 segment pairs from which we manually extracted paraphrases.

Finally, since we aim at detecting paraphrases between lay and specialized languages, we also looked at the relevance of the two types we chose to extract. That is, we evaluated the coherence of the results with our two initial hypotheses, which are expected to apply when both a specialized text segment and a lay text segment convey similar information: (1) nominalizations are more often used in specialized texts while lay texts tend to

[12]The lexicons used came from the Masson and Robert dictionaries.

[13]Stemming was performed using the Lingua::Stem perl package (http://search.cpan.org/~snowhare/Lingua-Stem-0.83) which is similar to the Snowball stemmers (http://snowball.tartarus.org)

	Specialized			Lay
(a)	N_s	...the benefits of *smoking cessation*...	N_l	...withdrawal symptoms of *smoking cessation*...
(b)	N_s	...regular *use of tobacco* concerned...	N_l	...*tobacco use* is the first cause...
(c)	N_s	...which goes with *smoking cessation*...	V_l	...who wants *to stop smoking*...

Table 2: Sample cases used to compute the conditional probability for nominalizations; (a) and (b) represent cases where a paraphrase was expected but did not occur and (c) a case where a paraphrase was indeed used. N = nominalization; V = verbal form.

	Specialized			Lay
(a)	C_s	...*glycemia* is lower...	C_l	...a drop of *glycemia*...
(b)	C_s	...the starting point of *thrombosis*...	C_l	...the risk of *thrombosis*...
(c)	C_s	...especially *cardiopathies* and...	M_l	...25% of *heart diseases*...

Table 3: Sample cases used to compute the conditional probability for neo-classical compounds; (a) and (b) represent cases where a paraphrase was expected but did not occur and (c) a case where a paraphrase was indeed used. C = compound; M = modern.

replace them with verbs; (2) specialized texts use more neoclassical compounds while lay texts give a paraphrase in modern language.

To evaluate (1) we measured the conditional probability $P(V_l|N_s)$ that a nominalization pattern N_s in a specialized segment be replaced by a matching verbal pattern V_l in a corresponding lay segment. These patterns are the paraphrasing patterns defined in Section 2.3.1 and exemplified in Table 1. Table 2 gives examples of cases taken into account when computing this probability, *i.e.* cases where both text segments convey the same information, as a nominalization in the specialized side and as a nominalization or a verbal paraphrase in the lay side. Formally, the probability can be estimated by $\frac{|Par_{N_s \to V_l}|}{|ExpPar_{N_s \to V_l}|}$, where $|Par_{N_s \to V_l}|$ is the number of correct extracted paraphrases involving a nominalization in a specialized segment and a verbal construction in the corresponding lay segment (case (c) of Table 2), and $|ExpPar_{N_s \to V_l}|$ the expected number of paraphrases. The expected number of paraphrases corresponds to the total number of instances where a specialized text segment contains a nominalization and the corresponding lay segment conveys the same information, expressed either as a nominalization or as a paraphrasing verbal construction (cases (a), (b) and (c) of Table 2). It is therefore computed as the sum of $|Par_{N_s \to V_l}|$ and $|Par_{N_s \to N_l}|$, the latter referring to the number of occurrences where both the specialized and lay segments match the same nominalization pattern, *i.e.*, instances where a paraphrase was expected but did not occur (cases (a) and (b) of Table 2). For instance *use of tobacco* on one side and *tobacco use* on the other side, as in (b), is a case where one would have expected a paraphrase such as *tobacco is used*. Note that matching allows the same flexibility as described in Section 2.3.1 in terms of synonyms and morphological variants. To test whether this tendency of using verbal constructions instead of nominalizations is indeed stronger in lay texts we also measured the reverse, *i.e.* the conditional probability $P(V_s|N_l)$, given a nominalization pattern N_l in a lay segment, that it be replaced with a matching verbal pattern V_s in the corresponding specialized segment, computed as $\frac{|Par_{N_l \to V_s}|}{|ExpPar_{N_l \to V_s}|}$. If our hypothesis is verified, this reverse probability should be lower then the direct probability.

In the same way, to evaluate (2) we measured the conditional probability $P(M_l|C_s)$ that a neo-classical compound C_s in a specialized segment be replaced by a modern-language equivalent M_l in a corresponding lay segment. Table 3 gives examples of cases taken into account when computing this probability, that is cases where both text segments convey the same information, as a neo-classical compound in the specialized side and as a neo-classical compound or a modern-language paraphrase in the lay side. Formally, it can be estimated by $\frac{|Par_{C_s \to M_l}|}{|ExpPar_{C_s \to M_l}|}$, where $|Par_{C_s \to M_l}|$ is the number of correct extracted paraphrases involving a neo-classical compound in a specialized

	Diabetes		Nicotine addiction		Cancer	
	S	L	S	L	S	L
docs	135	600	62	620	22	16
words	580,712	461,066	595,733	603,257	641,584	228,742
segment pairs	183		547		438	

Table 4: Sizes of the corpora (Number of documents, words and segment pairs; S=specialized, L=lay)

	Diabetes	Nicotine add.	Cancer
total paraph.	42	79	93
correct paraph.	30	62	62
precision	71.4%	78.5%	75.8%

Table 5: Precision for nominalization paraphrases (at the type level, not token level)

	Diabetes	Nicotine add.	Cancer
total paraph.	39	3	3
correct paraph.	24	3	3
precision	61.5%	100%	100%

Table 6: Precision for paraphrases of neo-classical compounds (at the type level, not token level)

segment and a modern-language equivalent in the corresponding lay segment (case (c) of Table 3) , and $|ExpPar_{C_s \to M_l}|$ is the expected number of paraphrases (case (a), (b) and (c) of Table 3). The expected number of paraphrases is the sum of $|Par_{C_s \to M_l}|$ and $|Par_{C_s \to C_l}|$, the latter referring to the number of occurrences where both the specialized and lay segments contains the same neo-classical compound (instances where a paraphrase was expected but did not occur, for instance cases (a) and (b) of Table 3). We then measured the reverse, *i.e.* the conditional probability $P(M_s|C_l)$, given a neo-classical compound C_l in a lay segment, that it be replaced with a modern-language equivalent M_s in the corresponding specialized segment, computed as $\frac{|Par_{C_l \to M_s}|}{|ExpPar_{C_l \to M_s}|}$.

3 Results

Table 4 gives size figures for each side (lay and specialized) of the three corpora in terms of documents, words and segment pairs.

Evaluation of the quality of the extracted paraphrases shows that precision is rather good for both type of paraphrases (see Tables 5 and 6), although the figures cannot be considered signicative for paraphrases of compounds extracted in the tobacco and cancer corpora given the small number of paraphrases (only 3 paraphrases in both cases).

Examples of nominalization paraphrases and paraphrases of neo-classical compounds are given in Tables 7 and 8. The last line of Table 7 shows an example of incorrect paraphrase, which is due to the synonymy link established between French words *charge* and *poids* which is not valid in that particular context. The last line of Table 8 also gives an incorrect example, which is caused by the imprecision of the modern-language paraphrase which is only partially equivalent to the neo-classical compound.

Specialized	Lay
consommation régulière *regular use*	consommer de façon régulière *to use in a regular fashion*
gêne à la lecture *reading difficulty*	empêche de lire *prevents from reading*
évolution de l'affection *evolution of the condition*	la maladie évolue *the disease is evolving*
*prise en charge *the taking care of*	prendre du poids *to take on weight*

Table 7: Examples of extracted nominalization paraphrases (* indicates an incorrect example)

With regard to the quantitative evaluation of the nominalization paraphrases, we measured a 30% recall on our sample of segment pairs, meaning that out of the 10 manually extracted paraphrases only 3 were automatically detected by our method. Cases of non-detected paraphrases were due to the restrained scope of the paraphrasing patterns, as well as to the presence of synonyms not contained

Specialized	Lay
leucospermie	Augmentation du nombre de globules blancs dans le sperme
leucospermia	*Increase in the number of white cells in the sperm*
glycémie *glycemia*	la quantité de sucre dans le sang *amount of sugar in the blood*
prostatectomie *prostatectomy*	l'ablation de la prostate *ablation of the prostate*
*hyperglycémie *hyperglycemia*	le taux de sucre dans le sang *proportion of sugar in the blood*

Table 8: Examples of extracted paraphrases of neo-classical compounds (* indicates an incorrect example)

in our lists.

Table 9 displays results for the investigation on the coherence of our first initial hypothesis that specialized texts use nominalizations where lay texts use verbal constructions. The conditional probability that a nominalization be replaced with a verbal construction is higher for nominalizations in specialized texts than for the reverse direction, which means that nominalizations in specialized texts are indeed more likely to be replaced by verbal constructions in lay texts than nominalizations in lay texts by verbal constructions in specialized texts. Results for the second hypothesis (neo-classical compounds in specialized texts tend to be replaced by modern-language equivalents in lay texts) are given in Table 10. As for the first hypothesis, the conditional probability for the neo-classical compounds in the specialized texts is higher, which seems to be coherent with the initial hypothesis. However, given the very small number of paraphrases, we cannot draw a significative conclusion as regards this second type of paraphrases.

4 Discussion

In this work we built comparable corpora of specialized and lay texts on which we implemented simple paraphrase acquisition methods to extract certain types of paraphrases that seemed relevant in the context of specialized and lay language: paraphrases based on nominalization vs. verbal constructions and paraphrases based on neo-classical compounds vs. modern-language expressions. The precision measured on the set of detected paraphrases is rather good, which indicates good quality of the paraphrases (hence of the paraphrasing patterns and extracted segments).

An originality of this work lies in the fact that, in contrast to approaches working with more closely related comparable corpora (Barzilay and Lee, 2003; Shinyama and Sekine, 2003; Elhadad and Sutaria, 2007), we also gathered comparable corpora of documents which, although addressing the same general topics (nicotine addiction, diabetes), were a priori rather different since coming from various sources and targeted to different populations. We showed that simple paraphrase acquisition methods could also work on documents with a lesser degree of similarity, once similar segments were detected. Indeed the precision of the extracted paraphrases is within the same range for the three corpora we built, despite the fact that one corpus (the cancer corpus) was composed of more similar documents than the other two.

We extracted a type of paraphrases much less exploited in existing work, with the exception of (Elhadad and Sutaria, 2007), that is paraphrases between specialized and lay language. This meant that we had to take into account what kind of paraphrases might be relevant, therefore the methods used to extract them were more constrained and supervised than approaches aiming at detecting any type of paraphrases. We based a part of our work on the hypothesis that among relevant types were paraphrases involving nominalizations of verbal contructions, meaning that lay texts tend to use verb phrases where specialized texts use deverbal noun contructions. Our results seem to support this hypothesis. Such paraphrases therefore seem to be interesting advice to give to authors of lay texts. Future work includes testing our method on English and comparing the results for the two languages. We would expect them to be fairly similar since the tendency to use nominal constructions in scientific literature has also been observed for English (Fang, 2005). The second part of our work exploited the hypothesis that lay texts use modern-language expressions where specialized texts use neo-classical compound words. In this case, the paraphrases were too few to enable us to draw a significative conclusion. Testing this method on different and larger corpora might give more insight into the relevance of extracting this type of paraphrases. As it is, this work is still experimental and needs to be further investigated.

	Diabetes		Nicotine addiction		Cancer	
	S→L	L→S	S→L	L→S	S→L	L→S
# paraphrases ($\|Par_{N_s \to V_l}\|$ or $\|Par_{N_l \to V_s}\|$)	44	37	140	76	73	57
# expected paraphrases ($\|ExpPar_{N_s \to V_l}\|$ or $\|ExpPar_{N_l \to V_s}\|$)	712	695	1675	1626	770	772
Conditional Probability ($P(V_l\|N_s)$ or $P(V_s\|N_l)$)	0.062	0.053	0.084	0.047	0.095	0.074

Table 9: Conditional probability for nominalization paraphrases in both directions, specialized-lay (S→L) and lay-specialized (L→S)

	Diabetes		Nicotine addiction		Cancer	
	S→L	L→S	S→L	L→S	S→L	L→S
# paraphrases ($\|Par_{C_s \to M_l}\|$ or $\|Par_{C_l \to M_s}\|$)	53	40	18	0	3	0
# expected paraphrases ($\|ExpPar_{C_s \to M_l}\|$ or $\|ExpPar_{C_l \to M_s}\|$)	686	675	196	178	1482	1479
Conditional Probability ($P(M_l\|C_s)$ or $P(M_s\|C_l)$)	0.074	0.059	0.092	0	0.002	0

Table 10: Conditional probability for paraphrases of neo-classical compounds in both directions

Its major drawback is the low number of paraphrases, in particular for the paraphrases of neo-classical compounds which brought inconclusive results. In order to gain insight on the low quantity of paraphrases of neo-classical compounds, we manually looked at sample text segments from the nicotine addiction and cancer corpora (the two corpora where very few paraphrases were extracted) and could not find any paraphrase of neo-classical compounds. This would seem to indicate that the low quantity of this type of paraphrases is due to the characteristics of the corpora rather than to defects of our extraction technique. As for the nominalization paraphrase, even though the method brought more paraphrases and gave encouraging results, their quantity is still quite small. The recall computed on a sample of segment pairs is low. This is mainly due to the fact that we set up rather rectricted paraphrasing patterns. This was done to ensure a high precision but caused the recall to fall. A future step would be to improve recall by modifying some aspects of the paraphrasing patterns while trying to keep a good precision.

Regardless of recall, the number of nominalization paraphrases in itself is also small. This can be due to the fact that we restrict ourselves to one specific type of paraphrases, but also to the facts that we first align and select similar text segments, that the coverage of our corpora might not be sufficient, and that we work on comparable corpora of lesser similarity than other methods. Future work to increase the number of paraphrases involves using clusters of text segments instead of pairs, increasing the corpus sizes and developing methods to detect other types of paraphrases besides the two kinds investigated here.

5 Conclusion

We presented a method based on comparable medical corpora to extract paraphrases between specialized and lay languages. We identified two kinds of paraphrases, nominalization paraphrases and paraphrases of neo-classical compounds, the first type seeming to indeed reflect some of the systematic differences between specialized and lay texts while the second type brought too few results to draw a signicative conclusion.

References

Colin Bannard and Chris Callison-Burch. 2005. Paraphrasing with bilingual parallel corpora. In *Proceedings of the 43rd Annual Meeting on Association for Computational Linguistics*, pages 597–604.

Regina Barzilay and Lillian Lee. 2003. Learning to paraphrase: An unsupervised approach using multiple-sequence alignment. In *HLT-NAACL*, pages 16–23, Edmonton, Canada.

Regina Barzilay and Kathleen McKeown. 2001. Extracting paraphrases from a parallel corpus. In *ACL/EACL*, pages 50–57.

Regina Barzilay. 2003. *Information Fusion for Multidocument Summarization: Paraphrasing and Generation*. Ph.D. thesis, Columbia University.

Yun-Chuang Chiao and Pierre Zweigenbaum. 2002. Looking for French-English translations in comparable medical corpora. In *Proc AMIA Symp*, pages 150–4.

Louise Deléger and Pierre Zweigenbaum. 2008a. Aligning lay and specialized passages in comparable medical corpora. In *Stud Health Technol Inform*, volume 136, pages 89–94.

Louise Deléger and Pierre Zweigenbaum. 2008b. Paraphrase acquisition from comparable medical corpora of specialized and lay texts. In *Proceedings of the AMIA Annual Fall Symposium*, pages 146–150, Washington, DC.

Noemie Elhadad and Komal Sutaria. 2007. Mining a lexicon of technical terms and lay equivalents. In *ACL BioNLP Workshop*, pages 49–56, Prague, Czech Republic.

Zhihui Fang. 2005. Scientific literacy: A systemic functional linguistics perspective. *Science Education*, 89(2):335–347.

Nabil Hathout, Fiammetta Namer, and Georgette Dal. 2002. An Experimental Constructional Database: The MorTAL Project. In *Many Morphologies*, pages 178–209.

Marti A. Hearst. 1997. Texttiling: Segmenting text into multi-paragraph subtopic passages. *Computational Linguistics*, 23(1):33–64.

Ali Ibrahim, Boris Katz, and Jimmy Lin. 2003. Extracting structural paraphrases from aligned monolingual corpora. In *Proceedings of the second international workshop on Paraphrasing*, pages 57–64, Sapporo, Japan. Association for Computational Linguistics.

Christian Jacquemin. 1999. Syntagmatic and paradigmatic representations of term variation. In *Proceedings of the 37th annual meeting of the Association for Computational Linguistics on Computational Linguistics*, pages 341–348, College Park, Maryland.

Adam Kilgarriff and Gregory Grefenstette. 2003. Introduction to the special issue on the web as corpus. *Computational Linguistics*, 29(3):333–47.

Aurélien Max. 2008. Local rephrasing suggestions for supporting the work of writers. In *Proceedings of GoTAL*, Gothenburg, Sweden.

Fiammetta Namer and Pierre Zweigenbaum. 2004. Acquiring meaning for French medical terminology: contribution of morphosemantics. In Marius Fieschi, Enrico Coiera, and Yu-Chuan Jack Li, editors, *MEDINFO*, pages 535–539, San Francisco.

Marius Pasca and Peter Dienes. 2005. Aligning needles in a haystack: Paraphrase acquisition across the web. In *Proceedings of IJCNLP*, pages 119–130.

Reinhard Rapp. 1995. Identifying word translations in non-parallel texts. In *Proceedings of the 33rd annual meeting on Association for Computational Linguistics*, pages 320–322.

Yusuke Shinyama and Satoshi Sekine. 2003. Paraphrase acquisition for information extraction. In *Proceedings of the second international workshop on Paraphrasing (IWP)*, pages 65–71, Sapporo, Japan.

An Extensible Crosslinguistic Readability Framework

Jesse Saba Kirchner
Department of Linguistics
UC Santa Cruz
1156 High Street
Santa Cruz, CA 95064
kirchner@ucsc.edu

Justin Nuger
Department of Linguistics
UC Santa Cruz
1156 High Street
Santa Cruz, CA 95064
jnuger@ucsc.edu

Yi Zhang
Baskin School of Engineering
UC Santa Cruz
1156 High Street, SOE 3
Santa Cruz, CA 95064
yiz@soe.ucsc.edu

Abstract

Automatic assessment of the readability level (i.e., the relative linguistic complexity) of documents in a large number of languages is an important problem that can be applied to many real-world applications, such as retrieving age-appropriate search engine results for kids, constructing automatic tutoring systems, and so on. Unfortunately, existing readability labeling techniques have only been applied to a very small number of languages. In this paper, we present an extensible crosslinguistic readability framework based on the use of parallel corpora to quickly create readability software for thousands of languages, including languages for which no linguists are available to define readability rules or for which documents with readability labels are lacking to train readability models. To demonstrate our idea, we developed a system based on the proposed framework. This paper discusses the theoretical and practical issues involved in designing such a system and presents the results of an experiment conducted with the system.

1 Introduction

Automatically labeling the reading difficulty of an arbitrary document is an important problem in several human language technology applications. It can, for example, be used in the next generation of personalized information retrieval systems to find documents tailored to children at different grade levels. In a tutoring system, it can be used to find online reading materials of the appropriate difficulty level for students (Heilman et al., 2006).

Of the world's more than 6,000 languages (Grimes, 2005), readability classification software exists for a striking few, and it is limited in coverage to languages spoken in countries with prominent standing in global economics and politics. A substantial number of the remaining languages nevertheless have a sufficient corpus of digital documents — a number which may already be in the hundreds and soon in the thousands (Paolillo et al., 2005). A natural idea is to create software to automatically predict readability levels (henceforth "RLs") for these documents. Such software has significant potential for applications in different areas of research, such as creating web search engines for kids speaking languages not covered by existing readability software, as described above.

There is much research on assessing the reading difficulties of texts in a particular language, and the existing work can be roughly classified as falling under two approaches. The first approach uses manually or semi-automatically crafted rules designed by computational linguists who are familiar with the language in question (Anderson, 1981). The second approach learns readability models for a particular language based on labeled data (Collins-Thompson and Callan, 2004).

Unfortunately, existing approaches cannot be easily extended to handle thousands of different languages. The first approach, using rules devised by computational linguists familiar with the languages, is impractical because for many languages, especially minority or understudied languages, there are relatively few linguists sufficiently familiar with the language to design such software. Even if these linguists exist, it is unlikely that a search engine company that wanted to serve the whole world would have the resources to

Proceedings of the 2nd Workshop on Building and Using Comparable Corpora, ACL-IJCNLP 2009, pages 11–18,
Suntec, Singapore, 6 August 2009. ©2009 ACL and AFNLP

hire all of them. The second approach, using machine learning techniques on labeled data, is very expensive because it requires the support of educated speakers of each language to provide readability labels for documents in the language. The availability of such speakers cannot always be assumed. Again, recruiting annotators for thousands of different languages is not economically feasible or practical for a company. An alternative strategy that can scale to thousands of different languages is needed.

In this paper, we propose a general framework to solve this problem based on a parallel corpus crawled from the web. To illustrate the idea, we developed an Extensible Crosslinguistic Readability system (henceforth "ECR system"), which uses a Cross-Lingual Information Retrieval (henceforth "CLIR") system that we call EXCLAIM. The ECR system functions to create RL classification software in any language with sufficient coverage in the CLIR system. We also report the promising — though very preliminary — results of an experiment that tests a real-world application of this system. Investigation of the basic assumptions and generalization of parameters and evaluation metrics are left for future work.

The rest of this paper is organized as follows. The problem setting is described in Section 2. The architecture of our ECR system is explained in Section 3. Our experimental design is laid out in Section 4, followed by experimental result analysis in Section 5. Section 6 gives an overview of related work, and section 7 concludes.

2 Problem and Proposed Methodology

2.1 Existing Approaches to Readability Classification

In traditional approaches to computational readability classification, there is a variety of language-specific system requirements needed in order to perform the RL classification task. For some languages, this task is relatively well-studied. For example, the simple and widely-used *Laesbarhedsindex* (henceforth "LIX") calculates RLs for texts written in Western European languages[1] with the following LIX formula:

$$RL_{\mathbb{D}} = \frac{\text{words}}{\text{sentences}} + \frac{100 \times \text{words}_{char>6}}{\text{words}}$$

[1]In practice, LIX may be substituted with other metrics, such as Flesch-Kincaid.

where $\mathbb{D}$ is a document written in an unfamiliar language, and $\text{RL}_{\mathbb{D}}$ is the readability score of the document D.

The above formula relies on specific parameters which have been tuned to a certain set of languages. These include the total number of words in $\mathbb{D}$ (words), the total number of sentences in $\mathbb{D}$ (sentences), and the total number of words in $\mathbb{D}$ with more than six characters ($\text{words}_{char>6}$).

Although this formula may be successful in RL classification for languages like English and French (Björnsson and Hård af Segerstad(1979), Anderson (1981)), it remains essentially parochial in the context of other languages because the parameters overfit the data from the Western Euorpean languages for which it was designed. Since the LIX formula depends on measuring the number of characters in a word to find words greater than 6, it is ineffective in determining the readability of documents written in languages with different writing systems, such as Chinese. This is due to the fact that some languages, like Chinese, are written with characters based on semantic meaning rather than phonemes, as in English, and a large number of Chinese words consist of just one or two characters, regardless of semantic complexity (Li and Thompson, 1981). In a similar vein, many languages of the world (even some that use phonemically-based writing systems) do not adhere to the implicit assumption of the LIX formula that semantically "complex" words are longer than simpler words (Greenberg, 1954). In these languages, then, the same metric cannot be used as a valid measure of RL difficulty of documents, since word length does not correlate with semantic complexity.

One recent alternative approach has been developed for readability labeling that uses multiple statistical language models (Collins-Thompson and Callan, 2004). The idea is to train statistical language models for each grade level automatically from manually labeled training documents. However, even an approach like this is not scalable to handle thousands of languages, since it is hard to recruit annotators of all of these languages to manually label the training data.

2.2 Proposed Solution

We propose a scalable solution to the problem of labeling the readability of documents in many languages. The general idea is to combine CLIR technology with off-the-shelf readability software for at least one well-studied language, such as English. First, off-the-shelf readability software is used to assign RLs to a set of documents in the source language, e.g. English, which serve as training data. Second, a set of key terms is selected from each group of documents corresponding to a particular RL to construct a readability model for that RL. Third, for each of these sets of terms, the cross-lingual query-expansion component of the CLIR system returns a semantically relevant set of terms in the target language. Finally, these target-language term sets are used to build the target-language RL models, which can be used to assign RLs to documents in the target language, even if language-specific readability classification software does not exist for that language. This solution plausibly extends to any of the languages covered by the CLIR system. It is possible to create a CLIR system by crawling the internet for parallel corpora, which exist for many language pairs. As a result, the proposed solution already has the potential to cover many different languages.

The success of this method relies on the assumption that readability levels remain fairly constant across syntactically and semantically parallel documents in the two languages in question, or simply across documents typified by equivalent key terms. This does not seem unreasonable: if the same information is represented in two different languages in semantically and structurally comparable ways, it is likely that the reading difficulty of the two texts should not differ much, if at all. If this assumption is true, generation of readability software really depends only on the availability of a solid CLIR system, and the problem of requiring trained computational linguists and native language speakers to design the system is mitigated.

Figure 1 shows a simple process model of a system for generating RL classifiers for various languages. A set of training documents from a source language (i.e., the "L1" in Figure 1) is assigned RLs by the off-the-shelf RL classification software R(L1). Using the source langauge files and the RLs produced by R(L1), the ECR system produces a source language (L1) readability model. Through the system interface, the CLIR system (EXCLAIM) uses the L1 readability model to produce a target language (L2) readability model. The system uses the L2 readability model to produce a new RL classifier R(L2) for the target language. The newly developed classifier R(L2) can then be used to classify documents in the L2.

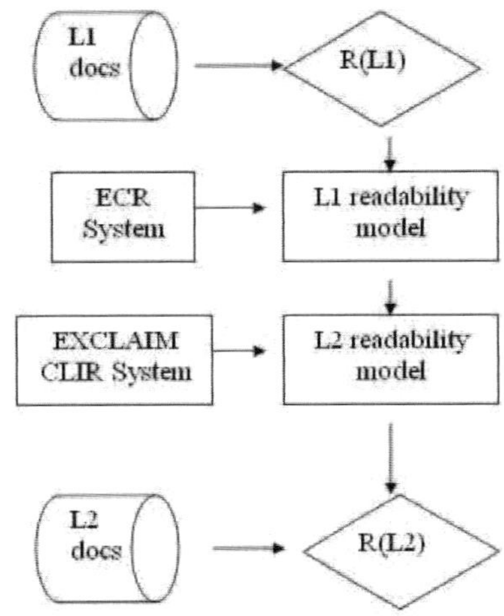

Figure 1: ECR Domain

3 System Architecture

To address any theoretical or empirical concerns and questions about the proposed solution, including those relating to the assumption that key term equivalence correlates with RL equivalence, we have developed an ECR system compatible with an existing CLIR system and have proposed evaluation metrics for this system. We developed the ECR system to meet the needs of two different kinds of users. First, higher-level *intermediate users* can build RL classification software for a given target language. Second, *end users* can use the software to classify documents in that language. In this section, we give a developer's-eye view of the system architecture (shown in Figure 2), making specific reference to the points at which intermediate and end users may interact with the system. For presentational clarity, we periodically adopt the arbitrary assumption that the source language is English, as this is the source language of our experiment described in the following section.

The ECR system has three primary tasks. The first task is to enable intermediate users to develop RL classification model for the source language. The second task is to provide the intermediate user with a toolkit to construct language-specific software that automatically tags documents in the target language with the appropriate RLs. The final task is to provide an interface module for the end

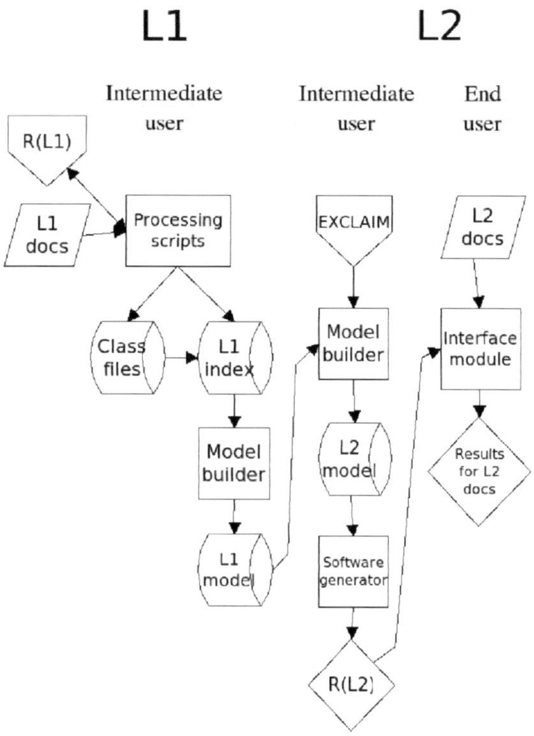

Figure 2: ECR System design

user to utilize this software.

In order to approach the first task, one needs a set of documents in a source language for which off-the-shelf readability software is available. This set of documents functions as a training data set; if a user is trying to assign RLs to documents in a particular domain — e.g., forestry, medical, leisure, etc. — then (s)he can already help shape the results of the system by providing domain-relevant source langauge data at this stage. To aid the intermediate user in obtaining RLs for this set of data, the ECR system has a number of parameters that may be selected, based on different models of RL-tagging — for example, we selected English as the source language and the aforementioned LIX formula due to its simplicity. The documents are then organized according to the generated RLs and separated into different RL groups.

At this point, the K most salient words are extracted from each source language RL groups ($RL_{\mathbb{S}}$) based on the following *tf*idf* term weighting:[2]

$$w_{i,j} = \left(0.5 + \frac{0.5\, freq_{i,j}}{max_l\, freq_{l,j}}\right) \times log\frac{N}{n_i}$$

[2]In principle, this choice is arbitrary and any other appropriate term-weighting formula could also be used.

The selected words $RL_{\mathbb{S}} = \{f_1, f_2, ... f_K\}$ form the basis for constructing an RL classification model for an unknown target language.

In order to construct a target language RL classification model, the cross-lingual query expansion component of a CLIR system is necessary to select semantically comparable and semantically related words in the target language. The CLIR system we developed is called EXCLAIM, or the **EX**tensible **C**ross-**L**inguistic **A**utomatic **I**nformation **M**achine. We constructed EXCLAIM from a semantically (though not structurally) parallel corpus crawled from Wikipedia (Wikimedia Foundation, 1999). All Wikipedia articles with both source and target language versions collectively function as data to construct the CLIR component. Due to Wikipedia's coverage of a large amount of languages (English being the language with the largest collection of articles at the time of writing), CLIR components for English paired with a wide number of target languages was created for EXCLAIM.

For each $RL_{\mathbb{S}}$, the query-expansion component of EXCLAIM determines a set of corresponding words for the target language $RL_{\mathbb{T}}$. Initially, each word in $RL_{\mathbb{S}}$ is matched with the source language document in EXCLAIM for which it has the highest *tf*idf* term weight. The M most salient terms in the corresponding target language document (calculated once again using the *tf*idf* formula) are then added to $RL_{\mathbb{T}}$. Therefore, $RL_{\mathbb{T}}$ contains no more than $K * M$ terms. The total set of $RL_{\mathbb{T}}$s form the base of the target language readability classification model.

Using this model, the system generates target language readability classification software on the fly, which plugs into the system's existing interface module for end users. Through the module, the end user can use the newly generated software to determine RLs for a set of target language documents without requiring any specialized knowledge of the languages or the software development process.

4 Experimental Design

We conducted an experiment to demonstrate this idea and to test our ECR system. Without loss of generality, we chose English as our source language and Chinese as our target language. While Chinese is a major language for which it would be relatively easy to find linguistic experts to write readability rules and native speakers to label document readability for training, our goal is not to demonstrate that the proposed solution is the best solution to build readability software for Chinese. Instead, we chose these languages for the following reasons. First, we are capable of reading both languages and are thus able to judge the quality of the ECR system. Second, publicly available English readability labeling software exists, and we are not aware of such software for Chinese. Third, we had access to a parallel set of documents that could be used for the evaluation of our experiment. Fourth, the many differences between English and Chinese might demonstrate the applicability of our system for a diverse set of languages. However, the features that made Chinese a desirable target language for us are not essential for the proposed solution, and do not affect the extensibility of the approach.

We created a test set using a collection of Chinese-English parallel documents from the medical domain (Chinese Community Health Resource Center, 2004). The set comprised 65 documents in English and their human-translated Chinese translations. Although a typical user does not need to have access to sets of bilingual documents for the system to run successfully, we circumvented both the lack of off-the-shelf Chinese readability labeling software and the lack of labeled Chinese documents for the evaluation of the results of our system by using a high quality translated parallel document set. Since RLs are rough measures of semantic and structural complexity, we assume they should be approximately if not exactly the same for a given document and its translation in a different language, an extension of the ideas in Collins-Thompson and Callan (2004). Based on this assumption, we can accurately compare the RLs of the translated CCHRC Chinese medical documents to the RLs of the original English documents, which we call the "true RLs" of the testing documents.

LIX-based RLs can be roughly mapped to grade levels, e.g., a text that is classified with an RL of 8 is appropriate for the average 8th grade reader. Since we can assign RLs to the English versions of the 65 CCHRC documents, these RLs can serve as targets to match when generating RLs for the corresponding Chinese versions of the same documents.

An advantage of our system arises from a complete vertical integration which allows a user with knowledge of the eventual goal to help shape the development of the target language RL classification model and software. In our case, the target language (Chinese) test set was from the medical domain, so we selected the OHSU87 medical abstract corpus as an English data set. We automatically classified the OHSU87 documents using the LIX mapping schema assigned by the UNIX *Diction and Style* tools,[3] given in the following Table.

LIX Index	RL	LIX Index	RL
Under 34.0	4	48.0-50.9	9
34.0-37.9	5	51.0-53.9	10
38.0-40.9	6	54.0-56.9	11
41.0-43.9	7	57.0 and over	12
44.0-47.9	8		

Table 1: Mapping of LIX Index scores to RLs as assigned by *Diction*

Then, we concatenated the English OHSU87 documents in each RL group. The *tf*idf* formula was used to select the K English words most representative of each RL group.

Next, we automatically selected a set of Chinese words for each RL class to create a corresponding Chinese readability model by passing each English word through the CLIR system, EXCLAIM, to retrieve the most relevant English document in the Wikipedia corpus, where relevance is measured using the *tf*idf* vector space model. The top M Chinese words from the corresponding Chinese document in the parallel Wikipedia corpus were added to $RL_{\mathbb{T}}$. By repeating this process for each word of each RL class, the Chinese readability model was constructed. In our experiment, we set $K = 50$ and $M = 10$ arbitrarily. The ECR system then automatically generated the subsequent RL classification software for Chinese.

Finally, we assigned a RL to each document in the test set. At this point the procedure is essentially similar to document retrieval task. Each RL group's set of words $RL_{\mathbb{T}}$ was treated as a document (d_j), and each test document to be labeled was treated as a query (q). RLs were ranked based on the cosine similarity between $RL_{\mathbb{T}}$ and q. Finally, the top-ranked RL was assigned to each test document.

[3] Available online at http://www.gnu.org/software/diction/diction.html.

5 Empirical Results

The results are presented below in Table 2. The RL assigned to each Chinese document is compared to the "true RL" of the English document, on the assumption that translation does not affect the readability level. Although only 7.8% of the RLs were predicted accurately (i.e., the highest ranked RL for the Chinese document corresponded identically to the RL of the translated English document), over 50% were either perfectly accurate or off by only one RL.

Correctly predicted RL	7.8%
RL off by 1 grade level	43.1%
RL off by 2 grade levels	18.4%
RL off by 3 grade levels	18.4%
RL off by 4 grade levels	6.1%
RL off by 5 grade levels	3.1%
RL off by 6 grade levels	0%
RL off by 7 grade levels	3.1%
RL off by 8 grade levels	0%

Table 2: Distribution of RLs as predicted by our ECR system

This table motivates us to represent the results in a more comprehensive fashion. Intuitively, the system tends to succeed at assigning RLs *near* the correct level, though not necessarily at the exact level. To quantify this intuition, we used Root Mean Squared Error (RMSE) to evaluate the experimental results. We compared our results to two kinds of baseline RL assignments. The first method was to randomly assign RLs 1000 times and take the average of the RMSE obtained in each assignment; this yielded an average RMSE of 3.05. The second method used a fixed equal distribution of the nine RLs, applying each RL to each document an equal number of times, and taking the average of these results. This baseline returned an average RMSE of 3.65. The average RMSE of our ECR system's performance on the CCHRC Chinese documents is 2.48. This number compares favorably against both of the baseline algorithms.

Recall that the actual RL-tagging procedure has been treated as a document retrieval task, using Vector Space Cosine similarity. As such, RLs are not simply "picked out" for each document: each document receives a cosine similarity score for each RL, calculated on the basis of its similarity to the language model word set constructed for each RL. For the results above, only the top ranked RL was considered, as this would be the RL yielded if the user wanted a discrete numeric value to assign to the text. If we allow for enough flexibility to select the better of the two top-ranked RLs assigned to each document by our ECR system, the results are as given in Table 3.

Correctly predicted RL	10.8%
RL off by 1 grade level	49.2%
RL off by 2 grade levels	27.7%
RL off by 3 grade levels	7.7%
RL off by 4 grade levels	1.5%
RL off by 5 grade levels	0%
RL off by 6 grade levels	3.1%
RL off by 7 grade levels	0%
RL off by 8 grade levels	0%

Table 3: RL Distribution (Best of Two Top-Ranked RLs)

While this extra selection is certain to improve the RMSE, what is surprising is the extent to which the RMSE improves. Once again, RMSE can be calculated in the following way. The two top-ranked RLs for each document are taken into consideration, and of these two RLs, the RL nearest to the true RL is selected. Selecting the best of the two top-ranked RLs causes the RMSE to drop to 1.91.

6 Related Work

The method described above builds on recent work that has exploited the web and parallel corpora to develop language technologies for minority languages (Trosterud (2002), *inter alia*).

Yarowsky et al. (2001) describe a system and a set of algorithms for automatically deriving autonomous monolingual POS-taggers, base noun-phrase bracketers, named-entity taggers, and morphological analyzers for an arbitrary target language. Bilingual text corpora are treated with existing text analysis tools for English, and their output is projected onto the target language via statistically derived word alignments. Their approach is especially interesting insofar as the system does not require hand-annotation of target-language training data or virtually any target-language-specific knowledge or resources.

Martin et al. (2003) present an English-Inuktitut aligned parallel corpus, demonstrating superior sentence alignment via Pointwise Mutual Information (PMI). Their approach provides broad coverage of cross-linguistic morphology, which has implications for dictionary expansion tasks; problems encountered in dealing with the agglutinative morphology of Inuktitut are suggestive of the myriad issues arising from cross-language comparisons.

Rogati et al. (2003) present an unsupervised learning approach to building an Arabic stemmer, modeled on statistical machine translation. The authors use an English stemmer and a small parallel corpus as training resources, with no parallel text necessary after the training phase. Additional monolingual texts can be incorporated to improve the stemmer by allowing it to adapt to a specific domain.

While Yarowsky et al. (2001), Martin et al. (2003) and Rogati et al. (2003) all focus on aligned *parallel* corpora, our approach differs in that we use *comparable* documents from Wikipedia are linked thematically on the basis of semantic content alone: there is no presumed structural or lexical alignment between parallel documents. We have adapted the methods used in conjunction with aligned parallel corpora for use with non-aligned parallel corpora to handle the task pursued by Collins-Thompson and Callan (2004), which presents a new approach to predicting the RLs of a document by evaluating readability in terms of statistical language modeling. Their approach employs multiple language models to estimate the most likely RL for each document.

This approach contrasts with other previous monolingual methods of calculating readability, such as Chall and Dale (1995), which assesses the readability of texts by calculating the percentage of terms that do not appear on a 3,000 word list that 80% of tested fourth-grade students were able to read. Similarly, Stenner et al. (1988) use the word frequency information from a 5-million-word corpus.

While our work has drawn from several techniques employed in prior research, we have mainly hybridized the technique of using parallel corpus employed by Yarowsky (2001) and the language modeling approach employed by Collins-Thompson and Callan (2004). Our approach relies on parallel corpora to build a readability classifier for one language based on readability software for another language. Rather than focusing on language-specific readability classification based on training data drawn from the same language as the testing data (Collins-Thompson and Callan, 2004), we have constructed a radically extensible tool that can easily create readability classifiers for an arbitrary target language using training data from a source language such as English. The result is a system capable of allowing a user to construct readability software for languages like Indonesian, for example, even if that user does not speak Indonesian — this is possible due to the large parallel English-Indonesian corpus on Wikipedia.

7 Conclusion

We have proposed a general framework to quickly construct a standalone readability classifier for an arbitrary (and possibly unfamiliar) language using statistical language models based both on monolingual and non-aligned parallel corpora. To demonstrate the proposed idea, we developed an Extensible Crosslingual Readability system. We evaluated the system on the task of predicting readability level of a set of Chinese medical documents. The experimental results show that the predicted RLs were correct or nearly correct for over 50% of the documents. This research is important because it is the only technique we are aware of that is capable of straightforwardly creating readability labels for hundreds, or theoretically even thousands, of different languages.

Although the general framework and architecture of the proposed system are straightforward, the details of implementation of the system modules could be further improved to achieve better performance. For example, all target language words are selected from a single "best-matching document" using EXCLAIM in this paper. Further experimentation might discover a better word selection module. Future work may also reveal delineation points for over- and under-specialized sets of training data. The OHSU87 data set was selected on the basis of its medical domain coverage, however it may not have provided broad enough coverage of the appropriate domain-independent vocabulary in the CCHRC documents. And finally, we conducted the experiment using our own CLIR system, EXCLAIM, while other CLIR systems might yield better results.

Acknowledgements

The research reported here was partly supported by NSF Grant #BCS-0846979 and the Institute of Education Sciences, US Department of Education, through Grant R305A00596 to the University of California, Santa Cruz. Any opinions, findings, conclusions or recommendations expressed in this paper are the authors', and do not necessarily reflect those of the sponsors.

References

Jonathan Anderson. 1981. Analysing the readability of English and non-English texts in the classroom with Lix. Paper presented at the Annual Meeting of the Australian Reading Association.

C. H. Björnsson and Birgit Hård af Segerstad. 1979. *Lix på Franska och tio andra språk*. Pedagogiskt centrum, Stockholms skolförvaltning.

Jeanne S. Chall and Edgar Dale. 1995. *Readability Revisited: The New Dale-Chall Readability Formula*. Brookline, Cambridge, Mass.

Chinese Community Health Resource Center. 2004. CCHRC Medical Documents. Retrieved December 9, 2006, from `http://www.cchphmo.com/cchrchealth/index_E.html`.

Kevyn Collins-Thompson and Jamie Callan. 2004. A language modeling approach to predicting reading difficulty. In *Proceedings of HLT/NAACL 2004*. ACL.

Joseph H. Greenberg. 1954. A quantitative approach to the morphological typology of language. In *Method and Perspective in Anthropology: Papers in Honor of Wilson D. Wallis*, pages 192–220, Minneapolis. University of Minnesota Press.

Barbara Grimes. 2005. *Ethnologue: Languages of the World, 15th ed.* Summer Institute of Linguistics.

Michael Heilman, Kevyn Collins-Thompson, Jamie Callan, and Maxine Eskenazi. 2006. Classroom success of an intelligent tutoring system for lexical practice and reading comprehension. In *Proceedings of the Ninth International Conference on Spoken Language Processing*.

Charles N. Li and Sandra Thompson. 1981. *Mandarin Chinese: A Functional Reference Grammar*. University of California Press.

Joel Martin, Howard Johnson, Benoit Farley, and Anna Maclachlan. 2003. Aligning and using an English-Inuktitut parallel corpus. In *Proceedings of the HLT-NAACL 2003 workshop on building and using parallel texts: Data driven machine translation and beyond*. ACL.

John Paolillo, Daniel Pimienta, and Daniel Prado. 2005. *Measuring Linguistic Diversity on the Internet*. UNESCO, France.

Monica Rogati, Scott McCarley, and Yiming Yang. 2003. Unsupervised learning of arabic stemming using a parallel corpus. In *Proceedings of the 41st annual meeting of the Association for Computational Linguistics*. ACL.

A.J. Stenner, I. Horabin, D.R. Smith, and M. Smith. 1988. *The Lexile Framework*. Metametrics, Durham, NC.

Trond Trosterud. 2002. Parallel corpora as tools for investigating and developing minority languages. In *Parallel corpora, parallel worlds*, pages 111–122. Rodopi.

Wikimedia Foundation. 1999. Wikipedia, the free encyclopedia. Retrieved May 8, 2006, from `http://en.wikipedia.org/`.

David Yarowsky, Grace Ngai, and Richard Wicentowski. 2001. Inducing multilingual text analysis tools via robust projection across aligned corpora. In *Proceedings of the First International Conference on Human Language Technology Research*, pages 161–168.

An Analysis of the Calque Phenomena Based on Comparable Corpora

Marie Garnier
CAS, Université Toulouse le Mirail
31000 Toulouse France
mhl.garnier@gmail.com

Patrick Saint-Dizier
IRIT-CNRS, 118, route de Narbonne,
31062 Toulouse France
stdizier@irit.fr

Abstract

In this short paper we show how Comparable corpora can be constructed in order to analyze the notion of 'calque'. We then investigate the way comparable corpora contribute to a better linguistic analysis of the calque effect and how it can help improve error correction for non-native language productions.

1 Aims and Situation

Non-native speakers of a language (called the target language) producing documents in that language (e.g. French authors like us writing in English) often encounter lexical, grammatical and stylistic difficulties that make their texts difficult to understand. As a result, the professionalism and the credibility of these texts is often affected. Our main aim is to develop procedures for the correction of those errors which cannot (and will not in the near future) be treated by the most advanced text processing systems such as those proposed in the Office Suite, OpenOffice and the like, or advanced writing assistance tools like Antidote. In contrast with tutoring systems, we want to leave decisions as to the proper corrections up to the writer, providing him/her with arguments for and against a given correction in case several corrections are possible.

To achieve these aims we need to produce a model of the cognitive strategies deployed by human experts (e.g. translators correcting texts, teachers) when they detect and correct errors. Our observations show that it is not a simple and straightforward strategy, but that error diagnosis and corrections are often based on a complex analytical and decisional process.

Most errors result from a lack of knowledge of the target language. A very frequent strategy for authors is to imitate the constructions of their native language so that the production resembles standard terms and constructions of the target language. This approach based on analogy is called a *calque* when surface forms are taken into consideration (Hammadou, 2000), (Vinay et al. 1963). The errors produced in this context may be quite complex to characterize, and they are often difficult to understand. When attempting to correct these errors, we find it interesting to have access to some of the characteristics of the native language of the author so that a kind of 'retro-analysis' of the error can be carried out. This would allow a much better rate of successful corrections, even on apparently complex errors involving long segments of words in a sentence.

Works on the correction of grammatical errors made by human authors (e.g. Writer's v. 8.2) have recently started to appear. These systems do not propose any explicit analysis of the errors nor do they help the user to understand them. The approach presented here, which is still preliminary, is an attempt to include some didactic aspects into the correction by explaining to the user the nature of her/his errors, whether grammatical or stylistic, while weighing the pros and cons of a correction, via argumentation and decision theories (Boutiler et ali. 1999), (Amgoud et ali. 2008). Persuasion aspects are also important within the didactical perspective (e.g. Persuation Technology symposiums), (Prakken 2006). Finally, the calque (direct copy) effect has been studied in the didactics of language learning, but has never received much attention in the framework of error correction, where a precise analysis of its facets needs to be conducted.

In this short document we present the premises of an approach to correcting complex grammatical and lexical errors based on an analysis of the calque effect. Calque effects cannot easily be reduced to the violation of a few grammar rules of the target language: they need an analysis of their

Proceedings of the 2nd Workshop on Building and Using Comparable Corpora, ACL-IJCNLP 2009, pages 19–22,
Suntec, Singapore, 6 August 2009. ©2009 ACL and AFNLP

own. For that purpose, we introduce several ways of constructing and annotating the forms calque effects can take in source and target language in bilingual corpora. These corpora are both relatively parallel, but also relatively comparable in the sense that they convey the same information even though the syntax is incorrect. From these annotations, different strategies can then be deployed to develop correction rules. The languages considered here are French, Spanish and English, which have quite rigid and comparable structures. We are investigating two other languages: Bengali and Thai, which have a very different structure (the former has a strong case structure and some free phrase order, the latter has a lot of optional forms and functions with a strong influence from context). Besides correcting errors, the goal is to make an analysis of the importance of the calque effect and its facets over various language pairs.

2 Constructing comparable corpora

2.1 General parameters of the corpora

The documents used to construct the corpora range from spontaneous short productions, with little control and proofreading, such as emails or posts on forums, wiki texts, personal web pages, to highly controlled documents such as publications or professional reports. Within each of these types, we also observed variation in the control of the quality of the writing. For example, emails sent to friends are less controlled than those produced in a professional environment, and even in this latter framework, messages sent to hierarchy or to foreign colleagues receive more attention than those sent to close colleagues. Besides the level of control, other parameters, such as target audience, are taken into consideration. Therefore, the different corpora we have collected form a continuum over several parameters (control, orality, audience, language level of the writer, etc.); they allow us to observe a large variety of language productions.

The analysis of errors has been carried out by a number of linguists which are either bilingual or with a good expertise of the target language. For each document, either a bilingual expert or two linguists which are respectively native speakers of the source language and target language were involved in the analysis, in order to guarantee a correct apprehension of the calque effect, together with a correct analysis of the idiosyncrasies and the difficulties of each language in the pair.

Calque effects cover a large range of phenomena. Here are three major situations, for the purpose of illustration:

(1) Lexical calque: occurs when a form which is specific to the source language is used; this is particularly frequent for prepositions introducing verb objects: *Our team participated to this project* where *in* should be used instead of *to*.

(2) Position calque: occurs when a word or a construction is misplaced. For example, in French the adverb is often positioned after the main verb whereas in English it must not appear between the verb and its object: *I dine regularly at the restaurant* should be *I regularly dine ....*

(3) Temporal calque: occurs for temporal sequences concerning the grammatical tenses of verbs in related clauses or sentences: *When I will get a job, I will buy a house* the future in French is translated into English by the present tense: *When I get a job.*

2.2 Scenarios for developing corpora

In (Albert et al. 2009), we present the different categories of errors encountered in the different types of documents we have studied, and the way they are annotated. These categories differ substantially according to text type. The approach presented below is based on this analysis.

In our effort to construct a corpus, we cannot use documents with several translations, such as notices or manuals written in several languages since we do not know how and by whom (human or machine) the translations have been done. In what follows, we present the two scenarios that seem to be the most relevant ones for our analysis.

A first scenario in constructing comparable corpora is simply to consider texts written by foreign authors, to manually detect errors (those complex errors not handled by text editors) and to propose a correction. Beside the correction, a translation of the alleged source text (what the author would have produced in his own language) is given. This study was carried out for the following pairs: French to English, French to Spanish and Spanish to English. So far, about 200 pages of textual document have been analyzed and tagged. The result is a corpus where the erroneous text segments are associated with a triple:

(1) the original erroneous segment, with the error category,

(2) the correction in the target language (since there may exist several corrections, the by-default correction is given first, followed by other, less prototypical corrections),
(3) the most direct translation of this segment into the author's native language, possibly a few alternatives if they are frequent. This translation is produced by a native speaker of a source language.

We have 22 texts representing papers or reports, about 20 web pages and about 80 emails or blog posts. These are produced by 55 different French authors, over a few domains: computer science, linguistics, health, leisure and tourism. Balance over domains and authors has been enforced as much as possible.

Here is an example based on our annotation schemas, mentioning some relevant attributes:
.... <error-zone error-type="future">
When I will get </error-zone>
<correction errror-rev="present">
When I get </correction>
<transl calque="future"> Quand j'aurais </transl>.....

A second scenario we are developing is to take existing texts in the source language, with a potentially high risk of calque effects, which are representative of the types of productions advocated above and of increasing difficulty, and to ask quite a large and representative population of users to translate these texts. Emails need to be translated in a short period of time while more formal texts do not bear any time constraints, so that authors can revise them at will. We then have a corpus which can be used to study how the calque effect functions and how it can optimally be used in automatic error correction.

In this latter scenario, important features are as follows:
Corpus: we built a set of short corpora (8 corpora), so that the task for each translator is not too long. Each corpus is about 5 pages long. It contains 2 pages of emails, some really informal and others more formal, 1 page in the style of a web page and 2 pages of more formal document (report, procedure, letter, etc.). Those texts are either real texts or texts we have slightly adapted in order to increase the potential number of calque effects.
Translators: we use a large population of translators (about 70), where the language competence is the major parameter. Age and profession are also noted, but seem to be less important. Each corpus is translated by 8 to 10 translators with different competences, so that we have a better understanding of the forms calques may take. Comptence is measured retroactively via the quality of their translations. For emails, translators are instructed to follow the provided text, possibly via some personal variation if they do not feel comfortable with the text. The goal is to improve naturalness (probably also in a later stage to study the forms of variations).
Protocol: in terms of timing, translators are asked to translate emails in a very short time span, which varies depending on the ability of the translator; conversely, they have as much time as needed for the other documents, which can be proofread over several days, as in real situations. No dictionary or online grammar is allowed.

3 Analysing the facets of the calque effect

Let us now briefly present how these corpora allow us to have a better linguistic analysis of the calque effect and how this analysis can help us improve error correction.

The first level of analysis is the evaluation of the importance of a calque error per category and subcategory. For the pair French to English, we are studying:

- lexical calques, among which: incorrect preposition, incorrect verb structure (transitive vs. intransitive uses), argument divergences (as for the verb to miss),
- lexical choice calques which account for forms used in English, which are close to French forms, but with different meanings *I passed an exam this morning* should be: *I took an exam this morning*, .
- structural calques, which account for syntactic structures constructed by analogy from French. In this category fall constructions such as the incorrect adverb position or the position of quite: *a quite difficult exercise* which must be *quite a difficult exercise*
- A few basic style calques, with in particular the problem of temporal sequence.

In terms of frequency, here are some examples of results related to calque effects, obtained from a partial analysis realized so far on 1200 lines of emails produced by about 35 different authors, for the pair French to English. Note that, in average,

emails have one error per line.
Lexical calques: incorrect lexical choice of preposition: 62, determiner: 30, adverbs: 12, modals: 26, incorrect idiomatic expression: 70.
Grammatical calques: incorrect position of adverbs: 38, adjectives: 7; argument omissions: 52, incorrect passive forms: 8.
Style: incorrect temporal sequences: 26, aspect: 20, punctuation: 76.

Alongside an evaluation of the distribution and frequency of the different categories of calque, in conjunction with the parameters considered in the corpus constitution (in particular foreign language level and type of document), we can analyze the evolution of the calque effect: when (i.e. at what language competence stage) and how they emerge, expand, and disappear. Another question is the analysis of the level of genericity of calques: some may be individual, related to the way a certain individual has experienced learning a foreign language, whereas some may be widespread among a certain linguistic population. Examining different document types is also interesting. It shows the performance of a subject when he must write hastily, with little control, in contrast with highly controlled productions. This allows us to analyze what remanence level of calques appear when the subject does not have the time to proofread his text, as opposed to those which are still present when he has time to proofread it. This also betrays a possible error hierarchy in the subject's mind, since the subject will be tempted to first correct the errors he thinks are the most important.

It is also interesting to take into consideration corpora over several language pairs, and in particular to contrast the French to English and Spanish to English pairs. Although French and Spanish are in the same language family, the calque effects observed are quite different. This is not surprising for a number of lexical calques, but more interesting for grammatical calques. For example, the grammar of pronouns and reflexives is quite different in Spanish, leading to forms such as *David is me*, a calque of *David soy yo*.

Finally, if we consider the two scenarios above, where the first one is probably a direct production in English, whereras the latter is a production via an explicit translation, it becomes clear that they require a different kind of effort. It is thus interesting to compare the frequency of the different calque categories encountered and their distribution over subjects. The translation from an explicit source is probably more constraining in terms of form and contents than text produced directly (or almost) in English. This is under investigation.

4 Perspectives

The work presented here is essentially the premises of a detailed analysis of the calque effect and, working on a language pair basis, on how this analysis can be used to substantially improve the performances of the correction for non trivial lexical and grammatical errors that current text editors cannot detect and correct. We have shown how corpora have been built. So far, they are quite small, but sufficient to make a preliminary and indicative analysis of the problems, and to suggest directions for research. These corpora are also too small to be used in any kind of statistical machine learning procedure to automatically correct errors.

Our goal is thus to propose some elements of a strategy for didacticians teaching foreign languages so that students can improve their performance, based on the knowledge of these effects.

References

Albert, C., Garnier, M., Rykner, A., Saint-Dizier, P., Analyzing a corpus of documents produced by French writers in English: annotating lexical, grammatical and stylistic errors and their distribution, Corpus Linguistics conference, Liverpool, 2009.

Amgoud, L., Dimopoulos, Y., Moraitis, P., Making decisions through preference-based argumentation. In Proceedings of the International Conference on Principles of Knowledge Representation and Reasoning (KR08), AAAI Press, 2008.

Boutilier, C., Dean, T., Hanks, S., Decision-theoretic planning: Structural assumptions and computational leverage. Journal of Artificial Intelligence Research, 11:194, 1999.

Chuquet, H., Paillard, M., Approche Linguistique des Problmes de Traduction, Paris, Ophrys, 1989.

Hammadou, J., The Impact of Analogy and Content Knowledge on Reading Comprehension: What Helps, What Hurts, ERIC, 2000.

Prakken, H., Formal systems for persuasion dialogue, Knowledge Engineering Review, 21:163188, 2006.

Vinay, Jean-Paul and Darbelnay, Jean: Stylistique Comparée du Francais et de l'Anglais, Paris, Didier, 1963.

Active Learning of Extractive Reference Summaries for Lecture Speech Summarization

Justin Jian Zhang and Pascale Fung
Human Language Technology Center
Department of Electronic and Computer Engineering
University of Science and Technology (HKUST)
Clear Water Bay,Hong Kong
{zjustin,pascale}@ece.ust.hk

Abstract

We propose using active learning for tagging extractive reference summary of lecture speech. The training process of feature-based summarization model usually requires a large amount of training data with high-quality reference summaries. Human production of such summaries is tedious, and since inter-labeler agreement is low, very unreliable. Active learning helps assuage this problem by automatically selecting a small amount of unlabeled documents for humans to hand correct. Our method chooses the unlabeled documents according to the similarity score between the document and the comparable resource—PowerPoint slides. After manual correction, the selected documents are returned to the training pool. Summarization results show an increasing learning curve of ROUGE-L F-measure, from 0.44 to 0.514, consistently higher than that of using randomly chosen training samples.

Index Terms: active learning, summarization

1 Introduction

The need for the summarization of classroom lectures, conference speeches, political speeches is ever increasing with the advent of remote learning, distributed collaboration and electronic archiving. These user needs cannot be sufficiently met by short abstracts. In recent years, virtually all summarization systems are extractive - compiling bullet points from the document using some saliency criteria. Reference summaries are often manually compiled by one or multiple human annotators (Fujii et al., 2008; Nenkova et al., 2007). Unlike for speech recognition where the reference sentence is clear and unambiguous, and unlike for machine translation where there are guidelines for manual translating reference sentences, there is no clear guideline for compiling a good reference summary. As a result, one of the most important challenges in speech summarization remains the difficulty to compile, evaluate and thus to learn what a good summary is. Human judges tend to agree on obviously good and very bad summaries but cannot agree on borderline cases. Consequently, annotator agreement is low. Reference summary generation is a tedious and low efficiency task. On the other hand, supervised learning of extractive summarization requires a large amount of training data of reference summaries. To reduce the amount of human annotation effort and improve annotator agreement on the reference summaries, we propose that active learning (selective sampling) is one possible solution.

Active learning has been applied to NLP tasks such as spoken language understanding (Tur et al., 2005), information extraction (Shen et al., 2004), and text classification (Lewis and Catlett, 1994; McCallum and Nigam, 1998; Tong and Koller, 2002). Different from supervised learning which needs the entire corpus with manual labeling result, active learning selects the most useful examples for labeling and requires manual labeling of training dataset to re-train model.

In this paper, we suggest a framework of reference summary annotation with relatively high inter labeler agreement based on the rhetorical structure in presentation slides. Based on this framework, we further propose a certainty-based active learning method to alleviate the burden of human annotation of training data.

The rest of this paper is organized as follows: Section 2 depicts the corpus for our experiments, the extractive summarizer, and outlines the acoustic/prosodic, and linguistic feature sets for representing each sentence. Section 3 depicts how to

Proceedings of the 2nd Workshop on Building and Using Comparable Corpora, ACL-IJCNLP 2009, pages 23–26,
Suntec, Singapore, 6 August 2009. ©2009 ACL and AFNLP

compile reference summaries with high inter labeler agreement by using the RDTW algorithm and our active learning algorithm for tagging extractive reference summary. We describe our experiments and evaluate the results in Section 4. Our conclusion follows in Section 5.

2 Experimental Setup

2.1 The Corpus

Our lecture speech corpus (Zhang et al., 2008) contains 111 presentations recorded from the NCMMSC2005 and NCMMSC2007 conferences for evaluating our approach. The manual transcriptions and the comparable corpus—PowerPoint slides are also collected. Each presentation lasts for 15 minutes on average. We select 71 of the 111 presentations with well organized PowerPoint slides that always have clear sketches and evidently aligned with the transcriptions. We use about 90% of the lecture corpus from the 65 presentations as original unlabeled data U and the remaining 6 presentations as held-out test set. We randomly select 5 presentations from U as our seed presentations. Reference summaries of the seed presentations and the presentations of test set are generated from the PowerPoint slides and presentation transcriptions using RDTW followed by manual correction, as described in Section 3.

2.2 SVM Classifier and the Feature Set

While (Ribeiro and de Matos, 2007) has shown that MMR (maximum marginal relevance) approach is superior to feature-based classification for summarizing Portuguese broadcast news data, another work on Japanese lecture speech drew the opposite conclusion (Fujii et al., 2008) that feature-based classification method is better. Therefore we continue to use the feature-based method in our work. We consider the extractive summarization as a binary classification problem, we predict whether each sentence of the lecture transcription should be in a summary or not. We use Radial Basis Function (RBF) kernel for constructing SVM classifier, which is provided by LIBSVM, a library for support vector machines (Chang and Lin, 2001). We represent each sentence by a feature vector which consists of acoustic features: duration of the sentence, average syllable Duration, F0 information features, energy information features; and linguistic features: length of the sentence counted by word and TFIDF information features, as shown in (Zhang et al., 2008). We then build the SVM classifier as our summarizer based on these sentence feature vectors.

3 Active Learning for Tagging Reference Summary and Summarization

Similar to (Hayama et al., 2005; Kan, 2007), we have previously proposed how presentation slides are used to compile reference summaries automatically (Zhang et al., 2008). The motivations behind this procedure are:

- presentation slides are compiled by the authors themselves and therefore provide a good standard summary of their work;
- presentation slides contain the hierarchical rhetorical structure of lecture speech as the titles, subtitles, page breaks, bullet points provide an enriched set of discourse information that are otherwise not apparent in the spoken lecture transcriptions.

We propose a Relaxed Dynamic Time Warping (RDTW) procedure, which is identical to Dynamic Programming and Edit Distance, to align sentences from the slides to those in the lecture speech transcriptions, resulting in automatically extracted reference summaries.

We calculate the similarity scores matrix $Sim = (s_{ij})$, where $s_{ij} = similarity(Sent_{trans}[i], Sent_{slides}[j])$, between the sentences in the transcription and the sentences in the slides. We then obtain the distance matrix $Dist = (d_{ij})$, where $d_{ij} = 1 - s_{ij}$. We calculate the initial warp path P: $P = (p_1^{ini}, ..., p_n^{ini}, ..., p_N^{ini})$ by DTW, where p_n^{ini} is represented by sentence pair(i_n^{ini}, j_n^{ini}): one from transcription, the other from slides. Considering that the lecturer often doesn't follow the flow of his/her slides strictly, we adopt Relaxed Dynamic Time Warping (RDTW) for finding the optimal warp path, by the following equation.

$$\begin{cases} i_n^{opt} = i_n^{ini} \\ j_n^{opt} = \underset{j=j_n^{ini}-C}{\overset{j_n^{ini}+C}{\operatorname{argmin}}} d_{i_n^{opt},j} \end{cases} \quad (1)$$

We consider the transcription sentences on this path as reference summary sentences. We then obtain the optimal path $(p_1^{opt}, ..., p_n^{opt}, ..., p_N^{opt})$, where p_n^{opt} is represented by (i_n^{opt}, j_n^{opt}) and C

is the capacity to relax the path. We then select the sentences i_n^{opt} of the transcription whose similarity scores of sentence pairs: (i_n^{opt}, j_n^{opt}), are higher than the pre-defined threshold as the reference summary sentences. The advantage of using these summaries as references is that it circumvents the disagreement between multiple human annotators.

We have compared these reference summaries to human-labeled summaries. When asked to "select the most salient sentences for a summary", we found that inter-annotator agreement ranges from 30% to 50% only. Sometimes even a single person might choose different sentences at different times (Nenkova et al., 2007). However, when instructed to follow the structure and points in the presentation slides, inter-annotator agreement increased to 80%. The agreement between automatically extracted reference summary and humans also reaches 75%. Based on this high degree of agreement, we generate reference summaries by asking a human to manually correct those extracted by the RDTW algorithm. Our reference summaries therefore make for more reliable training and test data.

For a transcribed presentation D with a sequence of recognized sentences $\{s_1, s_2, ..., s_N\}$, we want to find the sentences to be classified as summary sentences by using the salient sentence classification function $c()$. In a probabilistic framework, the extractive summarization task is equivalent to estimating $P(c(\overrightarrow{s}_n) = 1|D)$ of each sentence s_n, where $\overrightarrow{s}_n$ is the feature vector with acoustic and linguistic features of the sentence s_n.

We propose an active learning approach where a small set of transcriptions as seeds with reference summaries, created by the RDTW algorithm and human correction, are used to train the seed model for the summarization classifier, and then the classifier is used to label data from a unlabel pool. At each iteration, human annotators choose the unlabeled documents whose similarity scores between the extracted summary sentences and the PowerPoint slides sentences are top-N highest for labeling summary sentences. Formally, this approach is described in Algorithm 1.

Given document D: $\{s_1, s_2, ..., s_N\}$, we calculate the similarity score between the extracted summary sentences: $\{s_1^{'}, s_2^{'}, ..., s_K^{'}\}$ and the PowerPoint slide sentences: $\{ppts_1, ppts_2, ..., ppts_L\}$, by equation 2.

$$Score_{sim}(D) = \frac{1}{K}\sum_{n=1}^{K}\sum_{j=1}^{L} Sim(s_n^{'}, ppts_j) \quad (2)$$

4 Experimental Results and Evaluation

Algorithm 1 Active learning for tagging extractive reference summary and summarization

Initialization

For an unlabeled data set: U_{all}, $i = 0$

(1) Randomly choose a small set of data $X\{i\}$ from U_{all}; $U\{i\} = U_{all} - X\{i\}$

(2) Manually label each sentence in $X\{i\}$ as summary or non-summary by RDTW and human correction and save these sentences and their labels in $L\{i\}$

Active Learning Process

(3) $X\{i\} = null$

(4) Train the classifier $M\{i\}$ using $L\{i\}$

(5) Test $U\{i\}$ by $M\{i\}$

(6) Calculate similarity score of given document D between the extracted summary sentences and the PowerPoint slides sentences by equation 2

(7) Select the documents with top-five highest similarity scores from $U\{i\}$

(8) Save selected samples into $X\{i\}$

(9) Manually correct each sentence label in $X\{i\}$ as summary or non-summary

(10) $L\{i+1\} = L\{i\} + X\{i\}$

(11) $U\{i+1\} = U\{i\} - X\{i\}$

(12) Evaluate $M\{i\}$ on the testing set E

(13) $i = i + 1$, and repeat from **(3)** until $U\{i\}$ is empty or $M\{i\}$ obtains satisfying performance

(14) $M\{i\}$ is produced and the process ends

We start our experiments by randomly choosing six documents for manual labeling. We gradually increase the training data pool by choosing five more documents each time for manual correction. We carry out two sets of experiments for comparing our algorithm and random selection. We evaluate the summarizer by ROUGE-L (summary-level Longest Common Subsequence) F-measure (Lin, 2004).

The performance of our algorithm is illustrated by the increasing ROUGE-L F-measure curve in Figure 1. It is shown to be consistently higher than

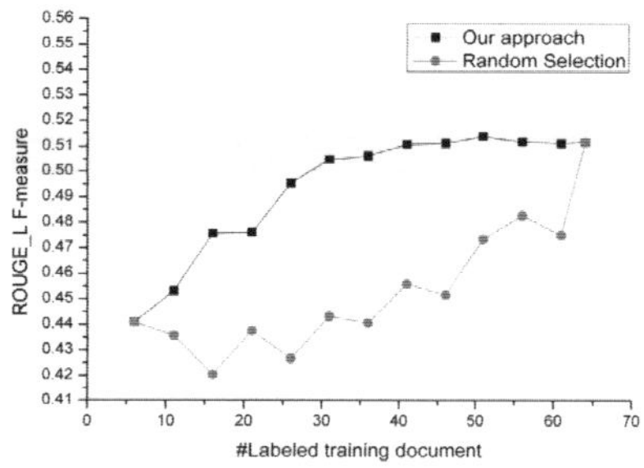

Figure 1: Active learning vs. random selection

using randomly chosen samples. We also find that by using only 51 documents for training, the performance of the summarization model achieved by our approach is better than that of the model trained by *random selection* using all 65 presentations (0.514 vs. 0.512 ROUGE-L F-measure). This shows that our active learning approach requires 22% less training data. Besides, acoustic features can improve the performance of active learning of speech summarization. Without acoustic features, our summarizer only performs 0.47 ROUGE-L F-measure.

5 Conclusion and Discussion

In this paper, we propose using active learning reduce the need for human annotation for tagging extractive reference summary of lecture speech summarization. We use RDTW to extract sentences from transcriptions according to PowerPoint slides, and these sentences are then hand corrected as reference summaries. The unlabeled documents are selected whose similarity scores between the extracted summary sentences and the PowerPoint slides sentences are top-N highest for labeling summary sentences. We then use an SVM classifier to extract summary sentences. Summarization results show an increasing learning curve of F-measure, from 0.44 to 0.514, consistently higher than that of using randomly chosen training data samples. Besides, acoustic features play a significant role in active learning of speech summarization. In our future work, we will try to apply different criteria, such as uncertainty-based or committee-based criteria, for selecting samples to be labeled, and compare the effectiveness of them.

6 Acknowledgements

This work is partially supported by GRF612806 of the Hong Kong RGC.

References

C.C. Chang and C.J. Lin. 2001. LIBSVM: a library for support vector machines. *Software available at http://www. csie. ntu. edu. tw/cjlin/libsvm*, 80:604–611.

Y. Fujii, K. Yamamoto, N. Kitaoka, and S. Nakagawa. 2008. Class Lecture Summarization Taking into Account Consecutiveness of Important Sentences. In *Proceedings of Interspeech*, pages 2438–2441.

T. Hayama, H. Nanba, and S. Kunifuji. 2005. Alignment between a technical paper and presentation sheets using a hidden markov model. In *Active Media Technology, 2005.(AMT 2005). Proceedings of the 2005 International Conference on*, pages 102–106.

M.Y. Kan. 2007. SlideSeer: A digital library of aligned document and presentation pairs. In *Proceedings of the 7th ACM/IEEE-CS joint conference on Digital libraries*, pages 81–90. ACM New York, NY, USA.

D.D. Lewis and J. Catlett. 1994. Heterogeneous uncertainty sampling for supervised learning. In *Proceedings of the Eleventh International Conference on Machine Learning*, pages 148–156. Morgan Kaufmann.

C.Y. Lin. 2004. Rouge: A Package for Automatic Evaluation of Summaries. *Proceedings of the Workshop on Text Summarization Branches Out (WAS 2004)*, pages 25–26.

A. McCallum and K. Nigam. 1998. Employing EM in Pool-based Active Learning for Text Classification. In *Proceedings of ICML*, pages 350–358.

A. Nenkova, R. Passonneau, and K. McKeown. 2007. The Pyramid Method: Incorporating human content selection variation in summarization evaluation. *ACM Transactions on Speech and Language Processing (TSLP)*, 4(2).

R. Ribeiro and D.M. de Matos. 2007. Extractive Summarization of Broadcast News: Comparing Strategies for European Portuguese. *Lecture Notes in Computer Science*, 4629:115.

D. Shen, J. Zhang, J. Su, G. Zhou, and C.L. Tan. 2004. Multi-criteria-based Active Learning for Named Entity Recognition. In *Proceedings of 42th Annual Meeting of the Association for Computational Linguistics*. Association for Computational Linguistics Morristown, NJ, USA.

S. Tong and D. Koller. 2002. Support vector machine active learning with applications to text classification. *The Journal of Machine Learning Research*, 2:45–66.

G. Tur, D. Hakkani-Tr, and R. E. Schapiro. 2005. Combining Active and Semi-supervised Learning for Spoken Language Understanding. *Speech Communications*, 45:171–186.

J.J. Zhang, S. Huang, and P. Fung. 2008. RSHMM++ for extractive lecture speech summarization. In *IEEE Spoken Language Technology Workshop, 2008. SLT 2008*, pages 161–164.

Train the Machine with What It Can Learn

– Corpus Selection for SMT

Xiwu Han
School of Computer Science and Technology,
Heilongjiang University,
Harbin City 150080 China
hxw@hlju.edu.cn

Hanzhang Li
School of Computer Science and Technology,
Heilongjiang University,
Harbin City 150080 China
lhj@hlju.edu.cn

Tiejun Zhao
School of Computer Science and Technology,
Harbin Institute of Technology,
Harbin City 150001 China
tjzhao@mtlab.hit.edu.cn

Abstract

Statistical machine translation relies heavily on available parallel corpora, but SMT may not have the ability or intelligence to make full use of the training set. Instead of collecting more and more parallel training corpora, this paper aims to improve SMT performance by exploiting the full potential of existing parallel corpora. We first identify literally translated sentence pairs via lexical and grammatical compatibility, and then use these data to train SMT models. One experiment indicates that larger training corpora do not always lead to higher decoding performance when the added data are not literal translations. And another experiment shows that properly enlarging the contribution of literal translation can improve SMT performance significantly.

1 Introduction*

Parallel corpora are generally considered indispensable for the training of a translation model in statistical machine translation (SMT). And most researchers tend to agree on the opinion that the more data is used to estimate the parameters of the translation model, the better it can approximate the true translation probabilities, and in turn this will lead to a better translation performance. However, even if large corpora are easily available, does an SMT system have the ability or intelligence to make full use of a training set?

Another aspect is that larger amounts of training data also require larger computational resources. With increasing quantities of training data, the improvement of translation quality will become smaller and smaller. Therefore, while continuing to collect more and more parallel corpora, it is also important to seek effective ways of making better use of available parallel training data.

Literal translation and free translation are two basic skills of human translation. A literal translation is a translation that follows closely the form of the source language, also known as word-for-word translation (Larson 1984).

According to Mona Baker (1992) translation needs to maintain equivalence at different levels across languages. In bottom-up sequence, these levels are: the word level, the above word level, the grammatical level, the textual level and the pragmatic level. Lower levels of equivalence are often embedded in literal translation and easily maintained, whereas higher levels are very important for free translation and very difficult to be achieved even for experienced translators because this kind of equivalence more often than not calls for thorough analysis and understanding of the source language, which is obviously what an SMT system cannot be capable of. So from this perspective SMT may be regarded as a beginner in learning how to translate.

The training of statistical machine translation mainly depends on the alignment probabilities estimated from certain frequencies observed in a parallel corpus. Thus, we may say that SMT translates according to its bilingual scanning experiences, and there is actually no deep comprehension during the coding and decoding process.

Since human learners of translation generally begin with the comparatively simpler techniques of literal translation, our efforts described in this paper are intended to discover whether a corpus

* This research is jointly supported by the National Natural Science Foundation of China under Grant No.60773069 and 60873169.

Proceedings of the 2nd Workshop on Building and Using Comparable Corpora, ACL-IJCNLP 2009, pages 27–33,
Suntec, Singapore, 6 August 2009.

©2009 ACL and AFNLP

of literal translations better suits the training of statistical machine translation.

In the following, section 2 introduces our corpus and proposes a combined method to recognize sentence pairs of literal translation. Section 3 describes our experiments with the acquired corpus on SMT training from two points of view. Section 4 analyzes the results from a linguistic point of view. And the conclusion is given in Section 5 with some suggestion for further work.

2 Literal Translation Recognition

Early machine translations were notorious for bad literal translations especially of idioms. However, good literal translation means to translate a sentence originally, and to keep the original message form, including the construction of the sentence, the meaning of the original words, use of metaphors and so on. Such a translation would be fluent and easy to comprehend by target language readers. If we suppose that the training corpus for SMT is mainly constituted of good translations, our first task is to identify those literally translated sentence pairs.

2.1 Our Corpus

The corpus used for our experiment consists of 650,000 bilingual sentence pairs of English and Chinese, which were gathered either from public and free Internet resources or from our own translation works. The sentences are either translated from Chinese to English or vice versa.

To facilitate the process of recognition, before the SMT experiment we preprocessed the corpus for the word and POS information, with English sentences parsed by (Collins 1999)'s head-driven parser and Chinese sentences by the head-driven parser of MI&TLAB at Harbin Institute of Technology (Cao 2006).

We define the literally translated sentence pairs as those that either embed enough word pairs which can be looked up in a bilingual dictionary, or share enough common grammatical categories. Hence, we invented two cross-lingual measures for the recognition of literal translation, i.e. lexical compatibility and grammatical compatibility.

2.2 Method of Lexical Compatibility

The seed version of our bilingual dictionary is made up of 63,483 entries drawn from the bilingual dictionary for the rule-based Chinese-English machine translation system of CEMT2K developed by MI&TLAB at Harbin Institute of Technology (Zhao 2001). We extended the seed with synonyms from English WordNet v. 1.2 and Chinese Extended Tongyicicilin v. 1.0. The extending algorithm is as follows.

Input: The seed version dictionary ***SD***, Chinese Extended Tongyicicilin ***CT***, and English WordNet ***EW***

Output: An extended Chinese English dictionary ***ED***

Do:

a. For each entry in ***SD***,
   a) extend the Chinese part with all its synonyms found in ***CT***;
   b) extend the English part with all its synonyms found in ***EW***;
   c) accept the extended entry into ***ED***.

b. For each entry in ***ED***,
   a) if its Chinese part is a subset of that of another entry, merge them;
   b) if its English part is a subset of that of another entry, merge them.

An entry in our final extended dictionary in turn is organized as bilingual synonym classes, and there are altogether 43,820 entries including 212,367 Chinese and English lexical terms.

By looking up Chinese-English word pairs in the extended dictionary, we defined the cross-lingual measure of lexical compatibility for a Chinese-English sentence pair as C_L.

$$C_L = \frac{\textit{the number of word pairs looked up}}{\textit{the total number of all words}}$$

For the recognition task, we employed a maximum likelihood estimation filtering method with an empirical threshold of 0.85 on the lexical compatibility. Sentence pairs would be accepted as literal translation if their lexical compatibility $C_L > 0.85$.

Manual analysis on 15,000 sentence pairs showed that for this method the precision is 94.65% and the recall is only 16.84%. The low recall is obviously due to the limitations of our bilingual dictionary.

2.3 Method of Grammatical Compatibility

Although the diversity of grammatical categories tends to be great, some common word classes, such as nouns, pronouns, verbs, adjectives, etc, mainly constitute the vocabularies of most natural languages. And our observations on English and Chinese parallel corpora show that the more literal a translation is, the more equivalent grammatical categories the pair of sentences may share.

We thus define the cross-lingual measure of grammatical compatibility as C_G.

$$C_G = \sum_{i=1}^{n} \lambda_i \frac{Min(|GE_i|, |GC_i|) + 1}{Max(|GE_i|, |GC_i|) + 1}$$

GE_i is an English grammatical category, $|GE_i|$ is the number it occurs in the English sentence, and GC_i is the Chinese counterpart (see Table 1). n is the number of common grammatical categories that make differences in the special task of recognizing literal translated sentence pairs. λ_i is the weight for the respective category, which is trained by a simple gradient descent algorithm on a sample of 10,000 manually analysed sentence pairs.

i	Chinese	English
1	noun	noun
2	pronoun	pronoun
3	verb	verb
4	adjective	adjective and adverb

Table 1: Equivalent grammatical categories

For the recognition task, we also employed a maximum likelihood estimation filtering method with an empirical threshold of 0.82 on the grammatical compatibility. Sentence pairs would be accepted as literal translation if their grammatical compatibility $C_G > 0.82$.

Evaluation on the held-out sample of 5,000 sentence pairs shows a precision ratio of 89.5% and a recall ratio of 42.34%.

2.4 Combination of the Two Methods

We simply combined the results of the two methods mentioned above to obtain a larger useful corpus. It is very interesting that the intersection between the results of the two methods accounts only for a very small part, which is estimated to be 17.2% of all the identified sentence pairs. The combined recognition results achieved a precision of 92.33% and a recall of 54.78% on the testing sample of 15,000 sentence pairs. And on the total corpus, our combined method acquired 201,062 sentence pairs that were classified to be the results of literal translation.

Further analysis on the sampled corpus shows that the wrongly unrecalled literally translated sentence pairs and the wrongly recalled ones are mainly due to bad segmentation of Chinese words or bad POS tagging results of both the Chinese and English parsers. In contrast, those sentence pairs correctly unrecalled are usually free transcriptions or bad translations.

3 SMT Experiments

3.1 Our Corpus and SMT System

After excluding some too long sentence pairs, we got our final training corpus, which includes 200,000 Chinese-English sentence pairs of literal translation and 400,000 pairs of free translation[1]. Our evaluation corpus was drawn from the IWSLT Chinese-to-English MT test set of 2004, which includes 506 Chinese sentences and 16 English reference sentences for each Chinese one.

Since our focus is not on a specific SMT architecture, we use the off-the-shelf phrase-based decoder Pharaoh (Koehn 2004). Pharaoh implements a beam search decoder for phrase-based statistical models, and has the advantages of being freely available and widely used. The phrase bilingual lexicon is derived from the intersection of bi-directional IBM Model 4 alignments, obtained with GIZA++ (Och and Ney 2003). For better comparison between experimental results, we kept all the system parameters as default, while only tuning our own parameters.

3.2 Experiment on Incremental Training Corpora

This experiment was designed to check whether it is true that larger training corpora always lead to better SMT decoding performance. We randomly segmented the 400,000 free translation sentence pairs into 4 subsets, with each of them including 100,000 pairs. A baseline SMT model was trained with the 200,000 literal translation sentence pairs, and then 4 other SMT models were trained on extended corpora, of which each later used corpus includes one more subset than the previous one.

The decoding performances in terms of BLEU and NIST scores of all 5 models are listed in the second and third column of Table 2, and the last column gives the numbers of out-of-vocabulary (OOV) words of each model on the test set. Curves in Figure 1 and 2, respectively, show the trajectories of BLEU and NIST scores in accordance with the sizes of extended training corpora.

[1] Note that "free translations" are identified statistically using our recognition method for literal translations.

Corpus Size	BLEU	NIST	OOV
200,000	0.3835	7.0982	47
300,000	0.3695	6.9096	45
400,000	0.4113	7.1242	32
500,000	0.4194	7.1824	21
600,000	0.4138	7.1566	18

Table 2: SMT performance with extended corpora

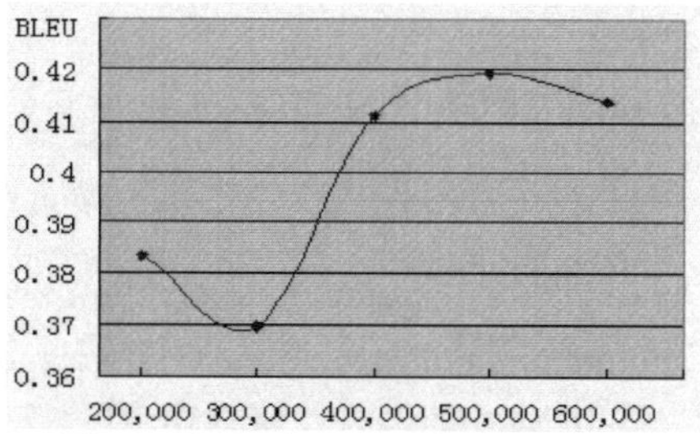

Figure 1: Trajectory of BLEU score

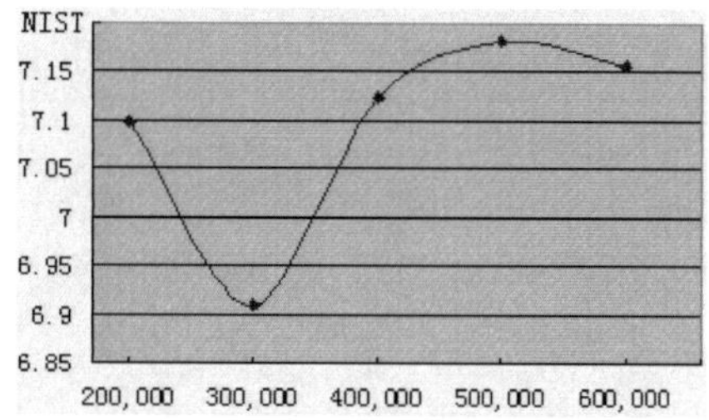

Figure 2: Trajectory of NIST score

A comparison between the different models' BLEU and NIST scores shows that a larger training data set does not necessarily lead to better SMT decoding performance. Based on the literal translation data, when more and more free translation data are added to the training set, the performance measures of the relevant SMT models fall at first, then rise, and at finally fall again. Furthermore, according to our manual analysis of the decoding results, free translation data have actually harmed the SMT model. It is just because the much smaller numbers of OOV words have made up for the impairment that the performance measures have risen for two times. They, however, will fall when the decrease in OOV words fails to make it up.

3.3 Experiment on Weighted Training Corpora

This experiment was designed to exploit both the contribution of literal translation and the advantage of a large vocabulary from a larger corpus. To achieve such a goal, minor modifications need to be made towards the training corpus and the module of GIZA++.

We start with an SMT training data set $\boldsymbol{X}$, which includes $\boldsymbol{n}$ bilingual sentence pairs, i.e. the input vector $\boldsymbol{X} = \{x_1, x_2, x_3, \ldots, x_i, \ldots, x_{n-1}, x_n\}$. During the original training process, every sentence pair $\boldsymbol{x_i}$ contributes in the same way to the estimation of parameters in the translation model since the corpus has not been weighted. Now we tried to adjust the contribution of $\boldsymbol{x_i}$ according to our previous decision whether it is literal translation or free translation. If we set the weight vector to be $\boldsymbol{W} = \{w_1, w_2, w_3, \ldots, w_i, \ldots, w_{n-1}, w_n\}^T$, the weighted corpus would become $\boldsymbol{X'} = \boldsymbol{WX} = \{w_1x_1, w_2\,x_2, w_3x_3, \ldots, w_ix_i, \ldots, w_{n-1}\,x_{n-1}, w_n\,x_n\}$, where

$$w_i = \begin{cases} \lambda & \text{when } x_i \text{ is literal translation,} \\ 1-\lambda & \text{otherwise.} \end{cases}$$

Hereby λ is an empirical weighting parameter in the range of $0 <= \lambda <= 1$.

The module of GIZA++ was modified to ensure that the weights imposed on sentence pairs could be effectively transmitted to smaller translation units. GIZA++ builds word alignments by means of counting occurrences of word pairs in the training corpus. Given a possibly translatable Chinese-English word pair $\boldsymbol{D} = <\boldsymbol{c}, \boldsymbol{e}>$, the number $\boldsymbol{N}$ of its occurrences in our original training corpus $\boldsymbol{X}$ can be calculated by summing up its occurrence number N_{xi} in each sentence pair, i.e.

$$N = \sum_{i=1}^{n} N_{xi}$$

Thus the weighted occurrence number $\boldsymbol{N'}$ of word pair $\boldsymbol{D}$ in the weighted training corpus can be calculated via the following equation.

$$N' = \sum_{i=1}^{n} N_{wi*xi} = \sum_{i=1}^{n} (w_i * N_{xi})$$

Finally, GIZA++ estimates word alignment parameters on the basis of $\boldsymbol{N'}$. Apart from this modification, all other parts of PHARAOH had been untouched to guarantee comparable experimental results.

We trained five SMT models of different weights on the previously mentioned corpora of free and literal translations. Table 3 lists both the training parameters and relevant decoding performances of the five models. Figures 3 and 4 show the trajectories of BLEU and NIST scores in accordance with the weight variable. We can see that the SMT model achieved the best performance when λ was set to be 0.67.

Corpus Size	λ	BLEU	NIST	OOV
400,000	0	0.4001	6.9082	23
600,000	0.5	0.4138	7.0796	18
600,000	**0.67**	**0.4259**	**7.2997**	**26**
600,000	0.8	0.4243	7.2706	39
200,000	1	0.3835	7.0982	47

Table 3: SMT performances with weighted corpora

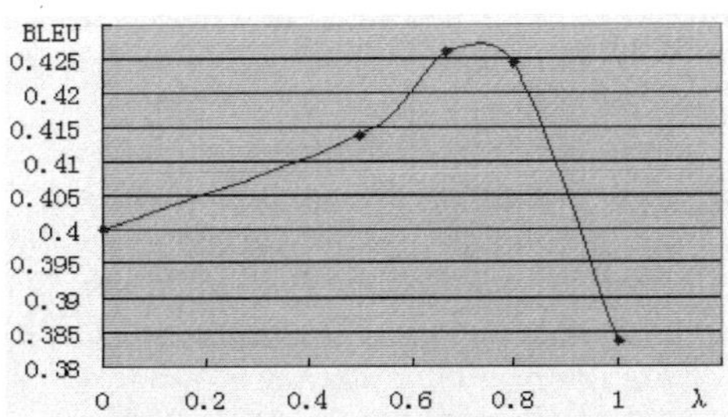

Figure 3: Trajectory of BLEU score

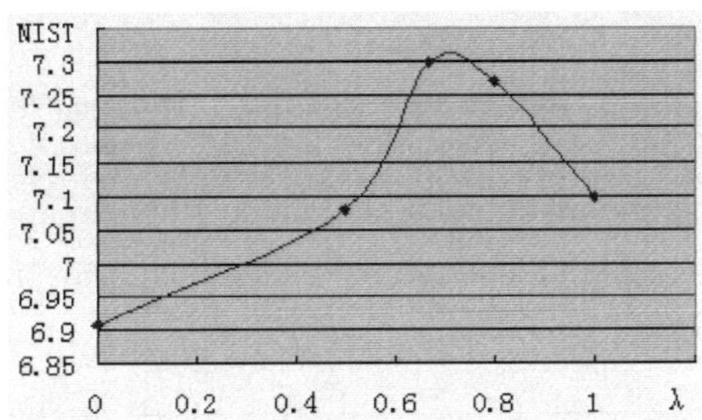

Figure 4: Trajectory of NIST score

Among the five models, that of $\lambda = 0.5$ is the baseline since here all sentence pairs contributed in the same way. Those of $\lambda = 0$ and 1 are two special cases designed to explore the isolated contribution of free and literal translation corpora in a contrastive way. Hereby the two models of $\lambda = 0.67$ and 0.8 are the central part of our experiment. According to the performance trajectories it seems that a reasonable increase in the contribution of the corpus of literal translations effectively improves the decoding performance of the SMT system since the BLEU scores with $\lambda = 0.67$ and 0.8 are higher than that of the baseline which are 0.0121 and 0.0105, and of the NIST scores which are 0.2201 and 0.191.

Our further analysis of the translation results and the related evaluation scores with different weight parameters showed that there exists some potential for literal translations to be used to improve SMT systems.

Our analysis indicates that two facts caused most of the out-of-vocabulary words (see Table 3). First, some OOV words never occurred in the training corpus; second, most others had been pruned off due to their much lower frequencies. Training corpora for $\lambda = 0.67$ and 0.8 have the same size of as that for $\lambda = 0.5$, but they resulted in much more OOV words than those for $\lambda = 0.5$ because the lower weight had decreased some related alignment probabilities very much. It seems that the large OOV increase must have counteracted the potential improvement to a certain degree although it did not have a devastating effects in these two cases. Therefore, a proper selection of a corpus of literal translations as training data would contribute more to the improvement of SMT models should some heuristic pruning methods be employed to avoid a possible OOV increase.

4 Related work

There have been a lot of studies on SMT training data. Most of them are focused on parallel data collections. Some work tried to acquire more parallel sentences from the web (Nie et al. 1999; Resnik and Smith 2003; Chen et al. 2004). Others extracted parallel sentences from comparable or non-parallel corpora (Munteanu and Marcu 2005, 2006). These works aim to collect more parallel training corpora, while our work aims to make better use of existing parallel corpora.

Some studies have also been conducted on parallel data selection and adaptation. Eck et al. (2005) proposed a method to select more informative sentences based on n-gram coverage. They used n-grams to estimate the importance of a sentence. The more previously unseen n-grams exist in the sentence, the more important the sentence is regarded. A TF-IDF weighting scheme was also tried in their method, but did not show improvements over n-grams. Their goal was to decrease the amount of training data to make SMT systems adaptable to small devices.

Some other works select training data according to domain information of the test set. Hildebrand et al. (2005) used an information retrieval method for translation model adaptation. They selected sentences similar to the test set from available in-of-domain and out-of-domain training data to form an adapted translation model. Lü et al. (2007) further used smaller adapted data to optimize the distribution of the whole training data. They took advantage both of larger data and adapted data.

Unlike all the above-mentioned studies, our method selected the training corpus according to basic theories of literal and free translation. This is somewhat similar to Lü et al. (2007), however, our weighting scheme also tried to make use of both larger and smaller data, which are free translations and literal translations in our case.

Besides, there have also been some studies on language model adaptation in recent years, motivated by the fact hat large-scale monolingual corpora are easier to obtain than parallel corpora.. Examples are Zhao et al. (2004), Eck et al. (2004), Zhang et al. (2006) and Mauser et al. (2006). Since a language model is built for the target language in SMT, a one pass translation is usually needed to generate the n-best translation candidates in language model adaptation. The principle in our research could also be used for translation re-ranking to further improve SMT performance.

5 Conclusions

This paper presents a new method to improve statistical machine translation performance by making better use of the available parallel training corpora. We at first identified literally translated sentence pairs by means of lexical and grammatical compatibility, and then used these data to train SMT models. Experimental results show that literal and free translation corpora contribute differently to the training of SMT models. It seems that literal translation training data better suit SMT system at its present level of intelligence. The weighted training data can further improve translation performance by enlarging the contribution of literal translations while maintaining a larger vocabulary from the larger corpus of free translations. Detailed analysis shows that a literal translation corpus would contribute more to the improvement of SMT models if some heuristic pruning methods would be employed to avoid possible OOV increase.

In future work, we will improve our methods in several aspects. Currently, the recognition method for literal translations and the weighting schemes are very simple. It might work better by trying some supervised recognition techniques or using more complicated methods to determine the weights of sentence pairs with variant literal degree. What's more, our present test corpus is an out-of-domain one, and this might have impacted the observations made in this work. Last, employing our method to the language model might also improve translation performance.

Acknowledgments

We are obliged to the authors of English WordNet version 1.2 and Chinese Extended Tongyicicilin version 1.0 for the free dictionary resources they provided. We also thank the two reviewers for their constructive advices that we referred to when preparing the last version of this paper.

References

Almut Silja Hildebrand, Matthias Eck, Stephan Vogel, and Alex Waibel. 2005. Adaptation of the Translation Model for Statistical Machine Translation based on Information Retrieval. *Proceedings of EAMT* 2005: 133-142.

Arne Mauser, Richard Zens, Evgeny Matusov, Sasa Hasan, Hermann Ney. 2006. The RWTH Statistical Machine Translation System for the IWSLT 2006 Evaluation. *Proceedings of International Workshop on Spoken Language Translation*: 103-110.

Bing Zhao, Matthias Eck, Stephan Vogel. 2004. Language Model Adaptation for Statistical Machine Translation with structured query models. *COLING-2004*.

Dragos Stefan Munteanu and Daniel Marcu. 2005. Improving Machine Translation Performance by Exploiting Comparable Corpora. *Computational Linguistics*, 31 (4): 477-504.

Dragos Stefan Munteanu and Daniel Marcu. 2006. Extracting Parallel Sub-Sentential Fragments from Comparable Corpora. *ACL-2006*: 81-88.

Franz Josef Och and Hermann Ney. 2003. A systematic comparison of various statistical alignment models. *Computational Linguistics*, 29(1): 19-52.

Hailong Cao. 2006. *Research on Chinese Syntactic Parsing Based on Lexicalized Statistical Model*, Dissertation for PhD, Harbin Institute of Technology, Harbin.

Jian-Yun Nie, Michel Simard, Pierre Isabelle, Richard Durand. 1999. Cross-Language Information Retrieval based on Parallel Texts and Automatic Mining of Parallel Texts in the Web. *SIGIR-1999*: 74-81.

Jisong Chen, Rowena Chau, Chung-Hsing Yeh. 2004. Discovering Parallel Text from the World Wide Web. *ACSW Frontiers 2004*: 157-161.

Matthias Eck, Stephan Vogel, and Alex Waibel. 2004. Language Model Adaptation for Statistical Machine Translation Based on Information Retrieval. *Proceedings of Fourth International Conference on Language Resources and Evaluation*: 327-330.

Michael Collins. 1999. *Head-Driven Statistical Models for Natural Language Parsing*. PhD Dissertation, University of Pennsylvania.

Mona Baker. 2000. *In Other Words: A Coursebook on Translaton*, Foreign Language Teaching and Research Press, Beijing.

Mildred L. Larson. 1984. *Meaning-based translation: A guide to cross-language equivalence*. Lanham, MD: University Press of America.

Philipp Koehn. 2004. Pharaoh: a beam search decoder for phrase-based statistical machine translation models. *In 6th Conference of the Association for*

Machine Translation in the Americas (AMTA), Washington, DC.

Philip Resnik and Noah A. Smith. 2003. The Web as a Parallel Corpus. *Computational Linguistics*, 29(3): 349-380.

Tiejun Zhao. 2001. *Technical Reports for CEMT2K.* MI&TLAB, Harbin Institute of Technology, Harbin.

Yajuan Lü, Jin Huang and Qun Liu. 2007. Improving Statistical Machine Translation Performance by Training Data Selection and Optimization. *Proceedings of the 2007 Joint Conference on Empirical Methods in Natural Language Processing and Computational Natural Language Learning*, pp. 343-350.

Ying Zhang, Almut Silja Hildebrand, Stephan Vogel. 2006. Distributed Language Modeling for N-best List Re-ranking. *EMNLP-2006*: 216-223.

Mining Name Translations from Comparable Corpora by Creating Bilingual Information Networks

Heng Ji
Computer Science Department, Queens College and the Graduate Center
The City University of New York, New York, NY, 11367, USA
hengji@cs.qc.cuny.edu

Abstract

This paper describes a new task to extract and align information networks from comparable corpora. As a case study we demonstrate the effectiveness of this task on automatically mining name translation pairs. Starting from a small set of seeds, we design a novel approach to acquire name translation pairs in a bootstrapping framework. The experimental results show this approach can generate highly accurate name translation pairs for persons, geo-political and organization entities.

1 Introduction

Accurate name translation is crucial to many cross-lingual information processing tasks such as information retrieval (e.g. Ji et al., 2008). Recently there has been heightened interest in discovering name pairs from comparable corpora (e.g. Sproat et al., 2006; Klementiev and Roth, 2006). By comparable corpora we mean texts that are about similar topics, but are not in general translations of each other. These corpora are naturally available, for example, many news agencies release multi-lingual news articles on the same day. There are no document-level or sentence-level alignments across languages, but important facts such as names, relations and events in one language in such corpora tend to co-occur with their counterparts in the other.

However, most of the previous approaches used a phonetic similarity based name transliteration module as baseline to generate translation hypotheses, and then exploit the distribution evidence from comparable corpora to re-score these hypotheses. As a result, these approaches are limited to names which are phonetically transliterated (e.g. translate Chinese name "*尤申科 (You shen ke)*" to "*Yushchenko*" in English). But many other types of names such as organizations are often rendered semantically, for example, the Chinese name "*解放之虎 (jie fang zhi hu)*" is translated into "*Liberation Tiger*" in English. Furthermore, many name translations are context dependent. For example, a person name "*亚西尔·阿拉法特*" should be translated into *"Yasser Arafat (PLO Chairman)"* or *"Yasir Arafat (Cricketer)"* based on different contexts.

Information extraction (IE) techniques – identifying important entities, relations and events – are currently available for some non-English languages. In this paper we define a new notion '*bilingual information networks*' which can be extracted from comparable corpora. An information network is a set of directed graphs, in which each node is a named entity and the nodes are linked by various 'attributes' such as hometown, employer, spouse etc. Then we align the information networks in two languages automatically in a bootstrapping way to discover name translation pairs. For example, after we extract bilingual

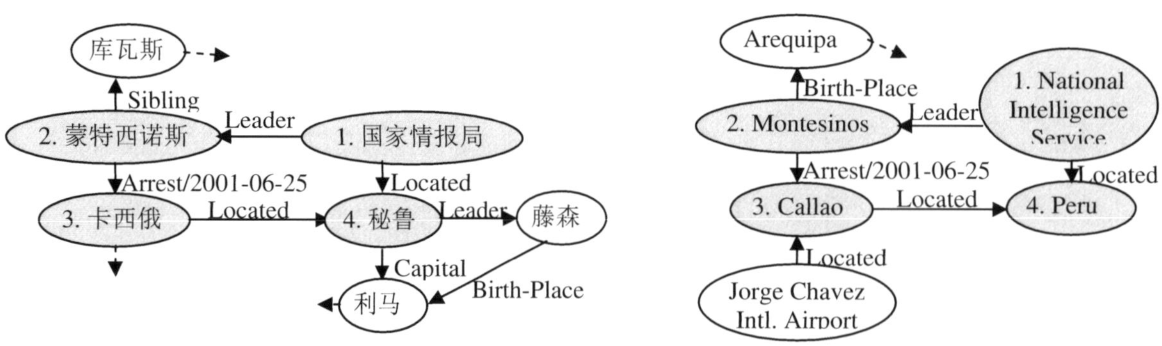

Figure 1. An example for Bilingual Information Networks

Proceedings of the 2nd Workshop on Building and Using Comparable Corpora, ACL-IJCNLP 2009, pages 34–37,
Suntec, Singapore, 6 August 2009. ©2009 ACL and AFNLP

information networks as shown in Figure 1, we can start from a common name translation "国家情报局-National Intelligence Service (1)", to align its *leader* as "蒙特西诺斯- Montesinos (2)", align the *arrest place* of Montesinos as "卡西俄-Callao (3)", and then align the *location* of Callao as "秘鲁-Peru (4)". Using this approach we can discover name pairs of various types (person, organization and location) while minimizing using supervised name transliteration techniques. At the same time, we can provide links among names for entity disambiguation.

2 General Approach

Figure 2 depicts the general procedure of our approach. The language pair that we are considering in this paper is Chinese and English. We apply IE techniques to extract information networks (more details in section 3), then use a bootstrapping algorithm to align them and discover name pairs (section 4).

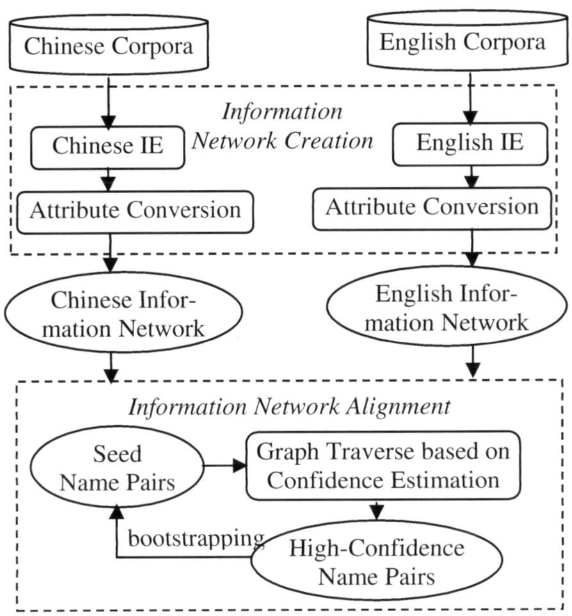

Figure 2. Name Translation Mining Overview

3 Information Network Creation

3.1 Bilingual Information Extraction

We apply a state-of-the-art bilingual information extraction system (Chen and Ji, 2009; Ji and Grishman, 2008) to extract ACE[1] types of entities, relations and events from the comparable corpora. Both systems include name tagging, nominal mention tagging, coreference resolution, time expression extraction and normalization, relation extraction and event extraction. Entities include persons, geo-political (GPE) and organizations; Relations include 18 types (e.g. "*a town some 50 miles south of Salzburg*" indicates a *located* relation.); Events include the 33 distinct event types defined in ACE05 (e.g. "*Barry Diller on Wednesday quit as chief of Vivendi*" indicates that "*Barry Diller*" is the *person argument* of a *quit* event occurred on *Wednesday*). The relation extraction and event extraction components produce confidence values.

3.2 Attribute Conversion

Then we construct a set of directed graphs for each language $G=\{G_i(V_i,E_i)\}$, where V_i is the collection of named entities, and E_i is the edges linking one name to the other, labeled by the attributes derived from the following two sources: (1) We select the relations with more static types to form specific attributes in Table 2[2], according to the entity types of a linked name pair. (2) For each extracted event we compose an attribute by combining its type and time argument (e.g. the "Arrest/2001-06-25" link in Figure 1). As we will see in the next section, these attributes are the key to discover name translations from the information networks because they are language-independent.

4 Information Network Alignment

After creating the information networks from each language, we automatically align them to discover name translation pairs. The general idea is that starting from a small seed set of common name pairs, we can rely on the link attributes to align their related names. Then the new name translations are added to the seed set for the next iteration. We repeat this bootstrapping procedure until no new translations are produced. We start from names which are frequently linked to others so that we can traverse through the information networks efficiently. For example, the seed set in processing ACE newswire data includes famous names such as "Indonesia", "China", "Palestine", "Sharon" and "Yugoslavia".

For each name pair <*CHName*, *EName*>, we search for all its related pairs <*CHName'*,

[1] http://www.itl.nist.gov/iad/mig//tests/ace/

[2] Many of these attributes are consistent with the definitions in NIST TAC-KBP task: http://apl.jhu.edu/~paulmac/kbp/090220-KBPTaskGuidelines.pdf

Name \ Name'	Person	Geo-political	Organization
Person	Spouse, Parent, Child, Sibling	Birth-Place, Death-Place, Resides-Place, Nationality	Schools-Attended, Employer
Geo-political	Leader	Located-Country, Capital	-
Organization	Leader	Location	-

Table 2. Relation-driven Attributes (Name → Name') in Information Network

Corpus \ Language	Chinese	English
ACE	CHSet1: XIN Oct-Dec 2000: 150 documents	ENSet1: APW Oct-Dec 2000: 150 documents ENSet2: AFP&APW Mar-June 2003: 150 documents
TDT-5	CHSet3: XIN Apr-Aug 2003: 30,000 documents	ENSet3: XIN Apr-Aug 2003: 30,000 documents ENSet4: AFP Apr-Aug 2003: 30,000 documents

Table 3. Number of Documents

ENName'>. Assuming *CHName* is linked to *CHName'* by an edge *CHEdge*, and *ENName* is linked to *ENName'* by *ENEdge*, then if the following conditions are satisfied, we align *CHName'* and *ENName'* and add them as seeds for the next iteration:

- *CHEdge* and *ENEdge* are generated by IE systems with confidence values higher than thresholds;
- *CHEdge* and *ENEdge* have the same attributes;
- *CHName'* and *ENName'* have the same entity type;
- If *CHName'* and *ENName'* are persons, the Damerau–Levenshtein edit distance between the pinyin form of *CHName'* and *ENName'* is lower than a threshold.

It's worth noting that although we exploit the pinyin information as essential constraints, this approach differs from the standard transliteration models which convert pinyin into English by adding/deleting/replacing certain phonemes.

5 Experimental Results

5.1 Data

We use some documents from the ACE (2004, 2005) training corpora and TDT-5 corpora to manually evaluate our approach. Table 3 shows the number of documents from different news agencies and time frames. We hold out 20 ACE texts from each language to optimize the thresholds of confidence values in section 4. A name pair <*CHName*, *EName*> is judged as correct if both of them are correctly extracted and one is the correct translation of the other in the certain contexts of the original documents.

5.2 Overall Performance

Table 4 shows the number and accuracy of name translation pairs discovered from CH-Set3 and EN-Set3, using 100 name pairs as seeds. After four iterations we discovered 968 new name translation pairs with accuracy 82.9%. Among them there are 361 persons (accuracy 76.4%), 384 geo-political names (accuracy 87.5%) and 223 organization names (accuracy 85.2%).

Iteration	1	2	3	4
Number of Name Pairs	205	533	787	968
Accuracy (%)	91.8	88.5	85.8	82.9

Table 4. Overall Performance

5.3 Impact of Time Frame and News Source Similarity

One major evidence exploited in the prior work is that the bilingual comparable corpora should be weakly temporally aligned. For example, Klementiev and Roth (2006) used the time distribution of names to re-score name transliteration. In order to verify this observation, we investigated how well our new approach can perform on comparable corpora with different time frames. Table 5 presents the performance of two combinations: CHSet1-ENSet1 (from the same time frame) and CHSet1-ENSet2 (from different time frames) with a seed set of 10 name pairs after 5 iterations.

Corpora	CHSet1-ENSet1	CHSet1-ENSet2
Number of Name Pairs	42	17
Accuracy (%)	81.0	76.5

Table 5. Impact of Time Frame Similarity

In addition, in order to measure the impact of news source similarity, we apply our approach to the combination of CHSet3 and ENSet4 which are from different news agencies. In total 815 name pairs are discovered after 4 iterations with overall accuracy 78.7%, which is worse than the results from the corpora of the same news source as shown in Table 4. Therefore we can clearly see that time and news source similarities are important to the performance of name translation pair mining.

5.4 Impact of IE Errors

Since in our approach we used the fully automatic IE pipeline to create the information networks, the errors from each component will be propagated into the alignment step and thus limit the performance of name translation discovery. For example, Chinese name boundary detection errors caused about 30% of the incorrect name pairs. As a diagnostic analysis, we tried to discover name pairs from CHSet1 and ENSet1 but with perfect IE annotations. We obtained 63 name pairs with a much higher accuracy 90.5%.

6 Related Work

Most of the previous name translation work combined supervised transliteration approaches with Language Model based re-scoring (e.g. Al-Onaizan and Knight, 2002; Huang et al., 2004). Ji et al. (2009) described various approaches to automatically mine name translation pairs from aligned phrases (e.g. cross-lingual Wikipedia title links) or aligned sentences (bi-texts). Our approach of extracting and aligning information network from comparable corpora is related to some prior work using comparable corpora to re-score name transliterations (Sproat et al., 2006; Klementiev and Roth, 2006).

In this paper we extend the target names from persons to geo-political and organization names, and extract relations links among names simultaneously. And we use a bootstrapping approach to discover name translations from the bilingual information networks of comparable corpora. In this way we don't need to have a name transliteration module to serve as baseline, or compute document-wise temporal distributions.

7 Conclusion and Future Work

We have described a simple approach to create bilingual information networks and then discover name pairs from comparable corpora. The experiments on Chinese and English have shown that this method can generate name translation pairs with high accuracy by using a small seed set. In the short term, our approach will provide a framework for many byproducts and directly benefit other NLP tasks. For example, the aligned sub-graphs with names, relations and events can be used to improve information redundancy in cross-lingual question answering; the outlier (mis-aligned) sub-graphs can be used to detect the novel or local information described in one language but not in the other.

In the future we plan to import more efficient graph mining and alignment algorithms which have been widely used for protein-protein interaction detection (Kelley et al., 2003). In addition, we will attempt using unsupervised relation extraction based on lexical semantics to replace the supervised IE pipeline. More importantly, we will investigate the tradeoff between coverage and accuracy by applying the generated name pairs to cross-lingual name search and machine translation tasks.

Acknowledgments

This material is based upon work supported by the Defense Advanced Research Projects Agency under Contract No. HR0011-06-C-0023 via 27-001022, and the CUNY Research Enhancement Program and GRTI Program.

References

Y. Al-Onaizan and K. Knight. 2002. Translating Named Entities Using Monolingual and Bilingual Resources. *Proc. ACL.*

Z. Chen and H. Ji. 2009. Language Specific Issue and Feature Exploration in Chinese Event Extraction. *Proc. HLT-NAACL.*

F. Huang, S. Vogel and A. Waibel. 2004. Improving Named Entity Translation Combining Phonetic and Semantic Similarities. *Proc. HLT/NAACL.*

H. Ji, R. Grishman, D. Freitag, M. Blume, J. Wang, S. Khadivi, R. Zens and H. Ney. 2009. Name Translation for Distillation. *Global Automatic Language Exploitation.*

H. Ji R. Grishman. 2008. Refining Event Extraction Through Cross-document Inference. *Proc. ACL.*

H. Ji, R. Grishman and W. Wang. 2008. Phonetic Name Matching for Cross-lingual Spoken Sentence Retrieval. *Proc. IEEE-ACL SLT.*

B. P. Kelley, R. Sharan, R. M. Karp, T. Sittler, D.E. Root, B. R. Stockwell and T. Ideker. 2003. Conserved pathways within bacteria and yeast as revealed by global protein network alignment. *The National Academy of Sciences of the United States of America.*

A. Klementiev and D. Roth. 2006. Named Entity Transliteration and Discovery from Multilingual Comparable Corpora. *Proc. HLT-NAACL.*

R. Sproat, T. Tao and C. Zhai. 2006. Named Entity Transliteration with Comparable Corpora. *Proc. ACL.*

Chinese-Uyghur Sentence Alignment: An Approach Based on Anchor Sentences

Samat Mamitimin
Xinjiang University
Urumqi 830046, China
Communication University of China/
Beijing 100024, China
tilchin@hotmail.com

Min Hou
Communication University of China
Beijing 100024, China
houminxx@263.net

Abstract

This paper, which builds on previous studies on sentence alignment, introduces a sentence alignment method in which some sentences are used as "anchors" and a two step procedure is applied. In the first step, some lexical information such as proper names, technical terms, numbers and punctuation marks, location information and length information are used to generate anchor sentences that satisfy some conditions. In the second step, texts are divided into several segments by using the anchor sentences as boundaries, and then the sentences in each segment are aligned by using a length-based approach. By applying this segmentation technique, the method avoids complex computation and error spreading. Experimental results show that the precision of the method is 94.6% on the average for Chinese-Uyghur sentence alignment for multi-domain texts.

1 Introduction

Parallel corpora are very useful for both theory-oriented linguistic research and application-oriented cross-language information processing. For parallel corpora, the most important annotation is alignment, especially sentence alignment, which is a minimal and essential requirement for the annotation of a parallel corpus. Aligning Chinese Uyghur parallel texts at the sentence level, however, is already very difficult because of the considerable differences in the syntactic structures and writing systems of the two languages.

A number of alignment techniques have been proposed for other language pairs, varying from statistical methods to lexical methods. There are basically three kinds of approaches on sentence alignment: the length-based approach (Gale and Church, 1991), the lexical approach (Kay and Röscheisen, 1993), and the combination of the two (Chen, 1993 and Wu, 1994).

The first approach is based on modeling the relationship between the lengths of sentences that are mutual translations. Similar algorithms based on this idea were developed independently by Brown, et al (1991) and Gale and Church (1993). However, their main targets are rigid translations that are almost literal translations. The method is applicable for structurally similar European languages (i.e. English-French or English-German).

One alternative alignment method is the lexicon based approach that uses lexical information to obtain higher accuracy. Kay and Röscheisen (1993) proposed a relaxation method to sentence alignment using the word correspondences acquired during the alignment process. Chen (1993) developed a method based on optimizing word translation probabilities which he showed gave better accuracy than the sentence-length based approach. Wu (1994) used a version of Gale and Church's method adapted to Chinese along with lexical cues in the form of a small corpus-specific bilingual lexicon to improve alignment accuracy in text regions containing multiple sentences of similar length. Melamed (1996) also developed a method based on word correspondences, for which he reported sentence-alignment accuracy slightly better than Gale and Church. The method does not capture enough word correspondences for structurally different languages such as Chinese and Uyghur, mainly for the following two reasons. One is the difference in the character types of the two languages. Chinese uses Chinese characters as its writing system while Uyghur uses alphabetic character. The other is the grammatical difference of the two languages. Chinese is an analytic language that has SVO word order. In contrast, Uyghur is

Proceedings of the 2nd Workshop on Building and Using Comparable Corpora, ACL-IJCNLP 2009, pages 38–45,
Suntec, Singapore, 6 August 2009. ©2009 ACL and AFNLP

a suffixing and agglutinative language that has SOV word order. Thus, it is impossible in general to apply the simple-feature based methods to Chinese-Uyghur sentence alignment.

This paper, on the basis of other sentence alignment methods, introduces an anchor sentence based sentence alignment method, in which some sentences are used as "anchors" and two steps are applied. In the first step, some lexical information such as proper names, technical terms, numbers and punctuation marks, location information and length information are used to generate anchor sentences that satisfy some conditions. In the second step, texts are divided into several segments by using anchor sentences as boundaries, and then the sentences in each segment are aligned by using a length-based approach.

2 The Chinese-Uyghur Parallel Corpus

Uyghur is a Turkic language spoken by Uyghur people in Xinjiang Uyghur Autonomous Region of China and adjoining areas, which has about 9 million speakers. As one of the official languages in Xinjiang, Uyghur is widely used in many fields such as education, communication, publication, etc. Bilingualism in Xinjiang requires translation from Chinese to Uyghur or in the opposite direction. Therefore, it is possible and essential to build a Chinese-Uyghur parallel corpus for teaching and research in translation, bilingual lexicography, linguistics, and other NLP applications. Consequently, we began to build a Chinese-Uyghur parallel corpus for linguistic research, translation studies, teaching and applications such as machine translation. The corpus is a sentence aligned general corpus of medium size.

So far, over 1 million characters of Chinese texts, in total 263 texts, and their corresponding Uyghur texts have been collected from several sources and included into the raw corpus after sampling. The corpus texts cover a variety of styles, such as fiction, scientific texts, government documents, law texts, daily conversation and other texts. Presently, the size of the corpus is smaller than we expected because it is not easy to obtain such digital text data which also needs to be processed before it can be included in the corpus. The main sources of text data are published books, news papers, magazines and some web pages. The proportions of the different genres in the corpus are shown in Figure 1.

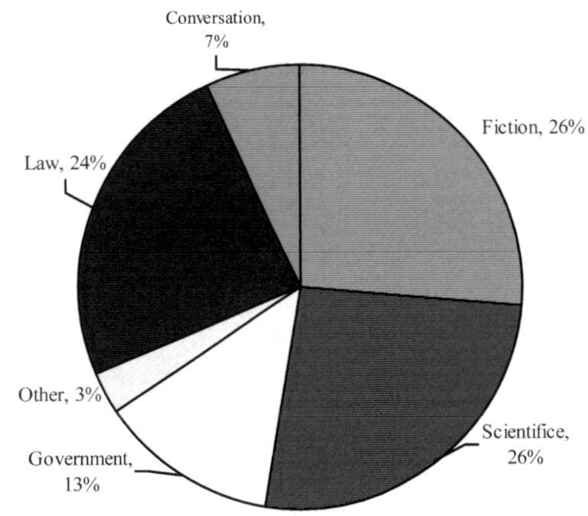

Figure 1. Genres and their percentages counted in tokens

3 System Overview

There is no previous work or approach specific to Chinese-Uyghur sentence alignment. So we firstly examined many papers related to the subject to find an appropriae method for Chinese-Uyghur sentence alignment. Most approaches share many common properties in the methods they use and suggest only small modifications to the earlier approaches. The length based method is suitable for aligning a very large bilingual corpus. Since it does not use any lexical information for the alignment task, it can be used between any pair of languages. However, in distant languages where characters differ, it is not so efficient. One alternative alignment method is the lexicon based approach that uses lexical information offering the potential for higher accuracy. However, it is not easy to capture enough word correspondences or cognates for Chinese and Uyghur. We may use bilingual dictionaries as an external resource to retrieve all possible word translations in such sentence alignment tasks. However, this is time-consuming and rather complex because word segmentation and lemmatization have to be done before the process of word matching can be started. Secondly, we tried some tentative methods to Chinese-Uyghur sentence alignment. According to the preliminary examination, it is generally not possible to apply the simple-feature based methods to Chinese-Uyghur sentence alignment.

Finally, we decided to apply a mixed approach to obtain better and more efficient results by combining the three criteria: length, lexical information and location information. Below are the detailed descriptions of this approach.

Our algorithm combines techniques adapted from previous work on sentence and word alignment. Our method is similar to Wu's (1994) in that it uses both sentence length and lexical information. But in our method, some lexical correspondences are used to find anchor sentences. Our method is similar to Simard's (1992) in that it uses cognates or anchors for sentence alignment. But in our method length information and anchors are used at different stages of sentence alignment. Our method is similar to Melamed's (1999) in that it uses a bitext mapping technique to locate anchor points, but it uses sentences as anchor points instead of words or characters. A segmentation technique that splits the text into several sections is also introduced to improve the length-based approach. As we can see from Figure 2, a two-step approach is applied to Chinese-Uyghur sentence alignment.

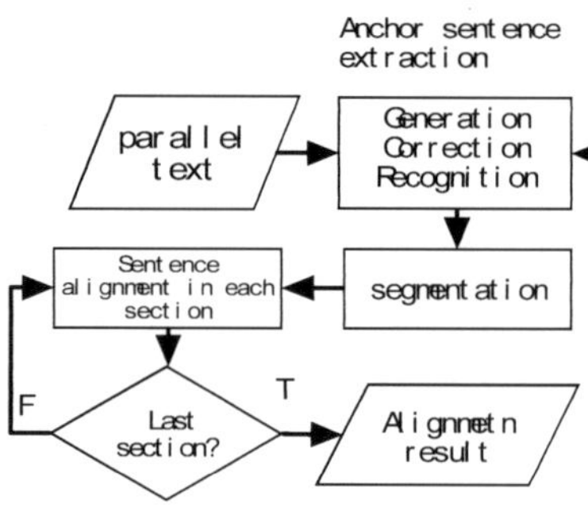

Figure 2: Flowchart of Chinese-Uyghur sentence alignment

In the first step, some (1:1) sentence pairs, called anchor sentences, are extracted by using lexical information, location and length information. A three-phase method is applied to anchor sentence extraction which will be explained in the following section.

In the second step, texts are divided into several segments by using these sentences as anchors, and then all sentences in each segment are aligned by using a length-based approach.

4 Anchor Sentence Extraction Algorithm

4.1 Anchor Sentence

Brown (1991) firstly introduced the concept of alignment anchors when he aligned the Hansard corpus. In our method, we also introduced this concept, which in our case are anchor sentences. In a parallel corpus, the anchor sentences are specific (1:1) sentence pairs that are strongly related and that satisfy some conditions. All such sentence pairs which were extracted from bilingual texts during the first step are seen as anchor sentences. These anchors divide the whole texts into short aligned segment. The goal of anchor sentence extraction is to divide the source text and the target text into one-to-one smaller segments. And using this segmentation, we attempt to improve the sentence alignments produced by the length based alignment. Sentence alignment tends to be better with shorter segments and, consequently, better sentence alignments are obtained.

For anchor sentence extraction, we applied a bitext mapping technique. A bitext map is a set of pairs (x, y), where x and y refer to precise locations in the first and second texts respectively, with the intention of denoting portions of the texts that correspond to one another (Simard, 1998). However, we used a bitext map of sentence pairs instead of words or characters to point out the correspondences between these anchor sentences (See Figure 3).

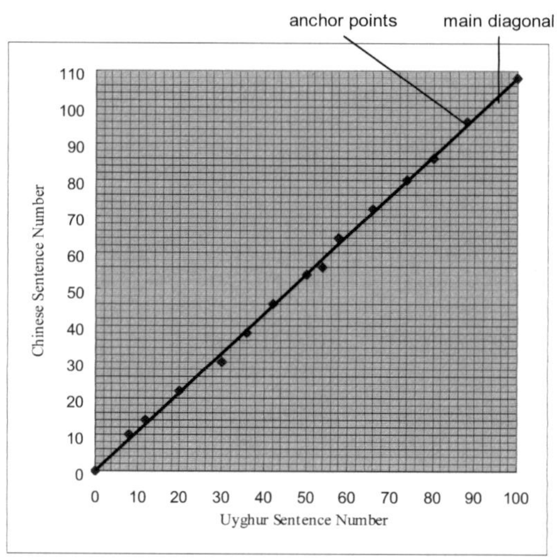

Figure 3. Bitext map of sentence alignments

The horizontal axis denotes the sentence number in the Uyghur text, and the vertical axis denotes the sentence number in the Chinese text. The anchor sentences, which are shown as anchor points in the bitext map, can be characterized by three properties:

Injectivity: no two anchor points in a bitext map can have the same x or y coordinates.

Linearity: anchor points tend to line up straight. In other words, all anchor points are to appear around a straight line.

Low variance of slope: The slope of the anchor points is rarely much different from the bitext slope.

4.2 Algorithm Description

In our anchor sentence extraction algorithm, a three-step process is applied to extract anchor sentences. In other words, the search for each anchor sentence pairs alternates between the following three steps: generation phase, correction phase and recognition phase.

- Generation phase

In the generation phase, the algorithm generates candidate anchor sentence points within a search rectangle. We define a search rectangle as follows: Rectangle(x, y, x+3, y+3) in which x=last anchor point(x) and y=last anchor point(y).

The first search rectangle is anchored at the origin of the bitext map where x=0, y=0. Subsequent search rectangles are anchored at the previously found points.

In this step, the search for an anchor sentence begins in a small search rectangle in the bitext map, whose diagonal is parallel to the main diagonal. If no candidate points are found, the search rectangle is proportionally expanded by the minimum possible amount, and the generation cycle is repeated. The rectangle keeps expanding until at least one acceptable point is found. Three kinds of information such as sentence length, location information and lexical information are used to generate anchor points. Sentence pairs that satisfy the following three conditions are added to the candidate anchor sentence array.

(1) Sentence length ratio

As was shown in the sentence alignment literature (Church, 1993), the sentence length ratio is also a very good indication of the alignment of a sentence pair.

In our method, for sentence pair P(c,u), if LenRatio(c,u)∈[MinLenRatio, MaxLenRatio], sentence pair P(c,u) would be candidate anchor sentences, in which LenRatio(c,u)= L_c/L_u (L_u is Uyghur sentence length, L_c is Chinese sentence length).

MinLenRatio and MaxLenRatio are calculated by using following formula:

MaxLenRatio=C′+A/(L_c+B)

MinLenRatio= C′-A (L_c+B)

C′=(C+ Len(C)/Len(U))/2

The constant C is the expected number of Chinese characters per Uyghur word. C′ is the weighted value when taking text size into account, the values of the constants are A=10, B=14.

(2) Matching score

If the matching score of a sentence pair is above the threshold (we set the threshold = 1.1), it is considered a candidate anchor sentence. By applying this condition, we reject some sentence pairs with a matching score smaller than the threshold. The matching score is calculated according to the matching degree of the key lexicon and punctuations as described in section 4.3.

(3) Maximum Angle Deviation (MAD)

According to the properties of the anchor sentences, the slope of the anchor points should not be much different from the bitext slope. So some sentence pairs are rejected by setting a maximum angle deviation. The angle of each anchor point's least-squares line is compared to the arc tangent of the bitext slope. The anchor point is rejected if the difference exceeds the maximum angle deviation threshold (MAD=3). The angle between the least-squares line and the bitext slope is calculated according to the following formula:

$$\theta = \arctan\left(\frac{|A-B|}{1+A*B}\right)$$

In this formula, A is the slope of the least-squares line, B is the bitext map slope.

This filtering process generates anchor sentences with higher accuracy; however, it causes errors in some cases. So, we introduced another correction phase in order to reject some wrongly aligned sentence pairs.

- Correction phase

In this step, some candidate sentences that are no anchor sentences are eliminated according to characteristics of anchor sentences, namely the length ratios of corresponding segments.

First, the algorithm checks if there are any conflicts between anchor points. The injective property of anchor sentences implies that whenever two anchor points overlap in the x or y axis, but are not identical in the region of overlap, then one of the points must be wrong. To resolve such conflicts, we employed a lookup method to eliminate conflicting points.

Secondly, length ratios of corresponding segments divided by candidate anchor sentences are calculated according to a similar formula as used for the sentence length ratio in order to reject wrongly aligned anchor points.

If the length ratio of the segments LenRatio(c,u)∈[MinLenRatio, MaxLenRatio], the candidate anchor sentence must be an anchor sentence, otherwise it should be eliminated. MinLenRatio and MaxLenRatio are calculated by using the following formulae:

$MaxLenRatio = C' + A/(L_c + B)$

$MinLenRatio = C' - A (L_c + B)$

- Recognition phase

A number of candidate anchor sentences can be obtained in a certain search region during application of the above two steps. For anchor sentence alignment, accuracy is more important than recall rate. So it is essential to introduce a recognition step in order to achieve higher accuracy by eliminating some unlikely anchor sentences. In the recognition step, one best anchor sentence pair is selected from candidate anchor sentences according to two parameters: matching score and length similarity score. The anchor selection algorithm gives a score to each proposed sentence pair during the recognition phase, and finds the alignment with the largest sum of scores. A parameter estimation method is described in the following section.

4.3 Parameter Estimation

Matching score: As previous work suggests, lexical information is critical for sentence alignment, especially for finding anchor points. It is well-known that some proper names and technical terms have rigid translations in many languages; numbers and punctuations appear in the same or similar forms in both source text and translation text. In a parallel text, for instance, if a sentence contains a question mark, it is likely to be aligned to a sentence that also contains this mark, which can be a strong clue for sentence alignment. This is also true for Chinese-Uyghur translations.

However, in our method, lexical and non-lexical clues are not used to align all sentences, but to estimate matching scores and to find the best anchor sentences. We used multiple clues such as proper names, technical terms, punctuation marks and numbers.

In most cases, proper names, including person names, location names, organization names, and technical terms have unique translations that will be matched easily. But, the problem is that person names and technical terms are often unknown words. How to identify them is a difficult problem. In our case, we first collected some popular proper names and the most frequent technical terms into a small lexicon that we call the key lexicon. More than 2000 words are included in the key lexicon at present. Then, a very simple searching method is applied to match corresponding words.

In addition, punctuation marks, including other symbols (e.g. @#$%&), are the most obvious clues in Chinese and Uyghur translation. The correlation between Chinese and Uyghur punctuations is extremely high as depicted in Table1.

Punctuation	Chinese	Uyghur
full stop	。	.
question mark	？	؟
exclamation mark	！	!
comma	，	،
ideographic comma	、	،
semicolon	；	؛
colon	：	:
quotation mark	“” ‘’	“” «» ‘’
bracket	（） []	() []
Title mark	《》	«»

Table 1. Corresponding punctuation marks in Chinese and Uyghur

For punctuation and numbers, no external resources but some rules are applied to estimate the matching degree of these clues.

The matching scores are calculated according to the average number of matched clues. In other words, the more matched proper names, technical terms, punctuation and numbers, the higher the matching score.

Length Similarity: Length similarity is a score that reflects the similarity between the length ratio of the current sentence pair and the expected length ratio. The following formula will be applied to calculate the length similarity of a proposed sentence pair (A_iC, A_iU):

$LenSimilar(A_iC, A_iU) = |Len(A_iC)/Len(A_iU) - C|/C$

Hereby C is expected number of Chinese character per Uyghur words. We obtain C=2.01 experimentally. $Len(A_iC)$ and $Len(A_iU)$ are the sentence lengths of A_iC, A_iU, respectively.

However, the sentence length ratio is not stable when a Chinese sentence is shorter than 10 characters. So it is necessary to add a weighting factor WF:

$LenSimilar(A_iC, A_iU) = |Len(A_iC)/Len(A_iU) - C|/C * WF$

if $Len(A_iC) <= StableLen$, then

$WF = a * Len(A_iC)/StableLen$, else WF =1.

Hereby StableLen=10, a=0.5

The length similarity formula is also adjusted as follows:

LenSimilar(A_iC,A_iU)=|Len(A_iC)/Len(A_iU)-C′|/C′* WF

Hereby C′ is the value weighted by the whole text size.

5 Length Based Sentence Alignment

According to previous work by Gale and Church, length-based approaches are simple and can achieve good performance for different language pairs. Because of this simplicity, many later researchers integrated this method to their sentence alignment methods. We also applied the length-based approach to the second step of sentence alignment.

5.1 Measuring Length in Words and Characters

Different length measuring methods can be used in the length-based approach. Brown (1991) introduced the length-based algorithm based on the number of *words* in sentences, Gail and Church's algorithm is similar to the Brown's algorithm except that alignment is based on the number of *characters* in the sentences.

Uyghur is an alphabetic language while Chinese is a non-alphabetic language. Therefore, it is a difficult problem to select the best length measuring model. In general, a Chinese sentence does not have word boundary information; so one way to define Chinese sentence length is to count the number of characters in a sentence. Another way is to count how many words are in a sentence after word segmentation. For Uyghur sentences, we can similarly define the length in characters or in words.

In our case, we examined three possible length models described in the following Table 2:

L-1	Both Uyghur and Chinese sentences are measured in *characters*
L-2	Both Uyghur and Chinese sentences are measured in *words*[1]
L-3	An Uyghur sentence is measured in *words* and a Chinese sentence is measured in *characters*

Table 2. Three length models

The mean sentence length ratios, variances and correlation coefficients for each of the length models are calculated from hand aligned Chinese-Uyghur texts of 988 sentence pairs. Statistics of the three sentence length models are shown in Table 3.

	L-1	L-2	L-3
Mean	3.99	1.07	2.01
Var	0.71	0.23	0.21
Correl	0.976	0.953	0.977

Table 3. Statistics of different length measuring methods

In general, the smaller the variance, the better the sentence length model should be. From Table 3, we can see that the character based length ratio model has significantly larger variance (0.71) than the other two models (L-2:0.23, L-3: 0.21). This means L-1 is not as reliable as L-2 and L-3. Both L-2 and L-3 have similar variance, but L-3 is better than L-2 with regard to the correlation coefficient, which indicates that sentence lengths have higher correlation if the lengths of Chinese and Uyghur texts are measured in characters and words, respectively. A regression analysis of the three models also proved this result. So we applied the L-3 model to the length ratio examination and length based sentence alignment.

5.2 Preliminary Statistics for the Length-based Method

A length-based sentence alignment program is based on a very simple statistical model of sentence lengths. The model makes use of the fact that longer sentences in one language tend to be translated into longer sentences in the other language, and that shorter sentences tend to be translated into shorter sentences. A probabilistic score is assigned to each pair of proposed sentence pairs, based on the ratio of lengths of the two sentences and the variance of this ratio. This probabilistic score is used in a dynamic programming framework in order to find the maximum likelihood alignment of sentences.

The parameters C and S^2 are used for likelihood estimation. C is the expected number of Chinese characters per Uyghur words. The parameters C and S^2 are determined empirically from a hand aligned parallel corpus of multi-domain texts. According to our statistical results, we obtained $C=2.01$ and $S^2=3.24$.

Brown (1991) assume that every parallel corpus can be aligned in terms of a sequence of minimal alignment segments, which they call "beads", in which sentences align 1-to-1, 1-to-2, 2-to-1, 2-to-2, 1-to-0, or 0-to-1. The alignment model is a generative probabilistic model for

[1] Bbibst software is used for Chinese word segmentation.

predicting the lengths of the sentences composing sequences of such beads. The model assumes that each bead in the sequence is generated according to a fixed probability distribution over bead types. We also calculated the probability of different alignment types.

Type	Frequency	Percentage (%)
1:1	807	81.3
1:0 or 0:1	5	0.5
1:2 or 2:1	152	15.3
2:2	7	0.7
1:3 or 3:1	20	2.0
other	2	0.2
Total	993	100

Table 4. Proportion of alignment types

From the above statistical results, it is clear that the correlation between the length of a Chinese sentence in characters and the length of its Uyghur translation sentence in words is extremely high. This high correlation suggests that length might be a strong clue for sentence alignment.
In our cases, we applied the length-based approach suggested by Gale and Church after some parameters had been changed.

6 Experimental Results

In this section, we report the results of experiments on aligning sentences by using two methods.

6.1 Test Corpus

In our experiment, we selected ten texts as our testing corpus. The texts are varied in length and genres as summarized in Table 2. T1, T2 and T3 are fiction texts; T4 is a law text; T5 and T6 are official documents; T7 and T8 are scientific texts, T9 and T10 are news and other articles. The total size of the corpus is 72,000 tokens, about 1300 sentence pairs.

6.2 Results

Firstly, we aligned sentences by using two approaches: a length-based algorithm, and an anchor sentence based algorithm. Then we manually checked the alignment results for errors and calculated precision and recall scores. Experimental results show that our anchor sentence based approach yields higher accuracy than the purely length based approach. The precision of the method is 94.6% on the average for Chinese-Uyghur sentence alignment on multi-domain texts. This is 2% higher than that of a purely length based approach.

	length-based		anchor sentence based	
	Precision	recall	precision	recall
T1	89.9	89.3	94.2	93.6
T2	94.9	94.9	97.5	97.5
T3	83.1	84.5	86.4	87.9
T4	100	100	100	100
T5	100	100	100	100
T6	98.8	98.8	100	100
T7	98.5	98.9	98.5	98.9
T8	65	66.7	72.5	74.4
T9	89.1	86.0	96.4	93.0
T10	96.8	95.8	94.7	93.8
average	92.7	92.8	94.6	94.8

Table 5. Experimental results

As we can see from Table 5, the error rates of the two methods vary from text to text. We analyzed all errors during sentence alignment in order to find reasons and solutions. The following is an error analysis.

6.3 Error Analysis

Firstly, the style of a text affects the sentence alignment results. In law texts and official documents, precision is very high in comparison with the results in texts of other styles; even 100% accuracy has been achieved. The reason for this may be the language style of source texts and translated texts. The error rate is comparatively higher in fiction texts because of their free translation style.

Secondly, complex sentence beads that include deletion and insertion during translation affect the alignment accuracy. According to Table 7, complex alignment types that the current alignment algorithm did not take into consideration account for 2.2% of the errors in Chinese-Uyghur translations. So errors caused by these "unorthodox" translation patterns are unavoidable. There are many such errors in sample T8. By examination, we found that the number of sentences in the Chinese text (122 sentences) and corresponding Uyghur text (179 sentences) is so unbalanced that many complex alignment types are involved. This is a direct reason for the high error rate.

Finally, anchor sentences play an important role during alignment. However, we found that it leads to more mistakes once wrong anchor sentence are selected. For instance, in T9, just one wrong anchor sentence caused up to four errors during second-step sentence alignment. So it is crucial to align anchor sentences correctly.

7 Conclusions

We have developed a very effective sentence alignment method based on anchor sentences. In our method, firstly anchor sentences are extracted from bilingual texts according to key lexical information, location information and length information; secondly, whole texts are divided into small segments by using anchor sentence points; finally, sentences in each small segment are aligned by using a length-based approach. We have implemented the proposed method on the parallel Chinese-Uyghur corpus. Experimental results show that the precision rate of the method is 2% higher than that of a purely length-base approach. Differences and advantages of our anchor sentence based method are compared to other methods in Table 6.

Methods	Length based	Lexical based	Our method	Advantages
Length information	Yes	No	Yes	Quick
Lexical information	No	Yes	Yes	Higher accuracy
Language resource	No	Dictionary	Simple lexicon	Simple
Special character	No	No	Yes	Higher accuracy
Multi level	No	No	Yes	Avoids error spreading
For multi-domain	Good	Not good	Good	Applicable to different texts

Table 6. Differences of three alignment methods

References

Brown, Peter, J. Lai and R. Mercer. 1991. Aligning Sentences in Parallel Corpora. *in Proceedings of ACL-91*, 169-176.

Brown, P.F., Della Pietra, S. A., Della Pietra, V. J., Mercer, R.L. 1993. The Mathematics of Statistical Machine Translation: Parameter Estimation. *Computational Linguistics,* 19(2): 263–311.

Chen, S.F. 1993. Aligning Sentences in Bilingual Corpora Using Lexical Information. *In Proceedings of ACL-91.*

Chuang, Thomas and Kevin C. Yeh. 2005. Aligning Parallel Bilingual Corpora Statistically with Punctuation Criteria. *International Journal of Computational Linguistics and Chinese Language Processing ,* Vol. 10, No. 1.

Gale, William A. and Kenneth W.Church. 1991. A Program for Aligning Sentences in Bilingual Corpora . *Proceedings of ACL-91*, 177-184.

Fung, Pascale and Kenneth W. Church. 1994. K-vec: A new approach for aligning parallel texts. *In Proceedings of the 5th International Conference on Computational Linguistics*, 1096-1102, Kyoto, Japan.

Kay, M., Röscheisen, M. 1993. Text-Translation Alignment. *Computational Linguistics*, 19(1): 121-142.

Melamed, I. D., Bitext Maps and Alignment via Pattern Recognition, *Computational Linguistics,* 25(1), 107-130, March, 1999.

Melamed, I.D. 1996. A Geometric Approach to Mapping Bitext Correspondence. IRCS Technical Report, 96-22, University of Pennsylvania.

Melamed, I.D. 1997. A Portable Algorithm for Mapping Bitext Correspondence. *In Proceedings of the 35th Annual Meeting of the Association for Computational Linguistics,* Madrid, Spain, 305-312.

Moore, R. C. (2002). Fast and Accurate Sentence Alignment of Bilingual Corpora. *In Machine Translation: From Research to Real Users* (Proceedings, 5th Conference of the Association for Machine Translation in the Americas, Tiburon, California), Springer-Verlag, Heidelberg, Germany, 135-244

Simard, M., Foster, G., and Isabelle, P. 1992. Using Cognates to Align Sentences in Bilingual Corpora. *Fourth International Conference on Theoretical and Methodological Issues in Machine Translation (TMI-92)*, Montreal, Canada.

Simard, M., Plamondon, P.1998. Bilingual Sentence Alignment: Balancing Robustness and Accuracy. *Machine Translation,* 13(1), 59–80.

Weigang Li, Ting Liu, Zhen Wang and Sheng Li. 1994. Aligning Bilingual Corpora Using Sentences Location Information, *Proceedings of 3rd ACL SIGHAN Workshop,* 141-147.

Wu, D. 1994. Aligning a Parallel English-Chinese Corpus Statistically with Lexical Criteria. *In Proceedings of the 32nd Annual Meeting of the Association for Computational Linguistics, Las Cruces,* New Mexico, 80-87.

Exploiting Comparable Corpora with TER and TERp

Sadaf Abdul-Rauf and **Holger Schwenk**
LIUM, University of Le Mans, FRANCE
Sadaf.Abdul-Rauf@lium.univ-lemans.fr

Abstract

In this paper we present an extension of a successful simple and effective method for extracting parallel sentences from comparable corpora and we apply it to an Arabic/English NIST system. We experiment with a new TERp filter, along with WER and TER filters. We also report a comparison of our approach with that of (Munteanu and Marcu, 2005) using exactly the same corpora and show performance gain by using much lesser data. Our approach employs an SMT system built from small amounts of parallel texts to translate the source side of the non-parallel corpus. The target side texts are used, along with other corpora, in the language model of this SMT system. We then use information retrieval techniques and simple filters to create parallel data from a comparable news corpora. We evaluate the quality of the extracted data by showing that it significantly improves the performance of an SMT systems.

1 Introduction

Parallel corpora, a requisite resource for Statistical Machine Translation (SMT) as well as many other natural language processing applications, remain a sparse resource due to the huge expense (human as well as monetary) required for their creation. A parallel corpus, also called bitext, consists in bilingual texts aligned at the sentence level. SMT systems use parallel texts as training material and monolingual corpora for target language modeling. Though enough monolingual data is available for most language pairs, it is the parallel corpus that is a sparse resource.

The performance of an SMT system heavily depends on the parallel corpus used for training. Generally, more bitexts lead to better performance. The existing resources of parallel corpora cover a few language pairs and mostly come from one domain (proceedings of the Canadian or European Parliament, or of the United Nations). The language jargon used in such corpora is not very well suited for everyday life translations or translations of some other domain, thus a dire need arises for more parallel corpora well suited for everyday life and domain adapted translations.

One option to increase this scarce resource could be to produce more human translations, but this is a very expensive option, in terms of both time and money. Crowd sourcing could be another option, but this has its own costs and thus is not very practical for all cases. The world wide web can also be crawled for potential "parallel sentences", but most of the found bilingual texts are not direct translations of each other and not very easy to align. In recent works less expensive but very productive methods of creating such sentence aligned bilingual corpora were proposed. These are based on generating "parallel" texts from already available "almost parallel" or "not much parallel" texts. The term "comparable corpus" is often used to define such texts.

A comparable corpus is a collection of texts composed independently in the respective languages and combined on the basis of similarity of content (Yang and Li, 2003). The raw material for comparable documents is often easy to obtain but the alignment of individual documents is a challenging task (Oard, 1997). Potential sources of comparable corpora are multilingual news reporting agencies like AFP, Xinhua, Al-Jazeera, BBC etc, or multilingual encyclopedias like Wikipedia, Encarta etc. Such comparable corpora are widely available from LDC, in particular the Gigaword corpora, or over the WEB for many languages and domains, e.g. Wikipedia. They often contain many sentences that are reasonable translations of

Proceedings of the 2nd Workshop on Building and Using Comparable Corpora, ACL-IJCNLP 2009, pages 46–54,
Suntec, Singapore, 6 August 2009. ©2009 ACL and AFNLP

each other. Reliable identification of these pairs would enable the automatic creation of large and diverse parallel corpora.

The ease of availability of these comparable corpora and the potential for parallel corpus as well as dictionary creation has sparked an interest in trying to make maximum use of these comparable resources, some of these works include dictionary learning and identifying word translations (Rapp, 1995), named entity recognition (Sproat et al., 2006), word sense disambiguation (Kaji, 2003), improving SMT performance using extracted parallel sentences (Munteanu and Marcu, 2005), (Rauf and Schwenk, 2009). There has been considerable amount of work on bilingual comparable corpora to learn word translations as well as discovering parallel sentences. Yang and Lee (2003) use an approach based on dynamic programming to identify potential parallel sentences in title pairs. Longest common sub sequence, edit operations and match-based score functions are subsequently used to determine confidence scores. Resnik and Smith (2003) propose their STRAND web-mining based system and show that their approach is able to find large numbers of similar document pairs.

Works aimed at discovering parallel sentences include (Utiyama and Isahara, 2003), who use cross-language information retrieval techniques and dynamic programming to extract sentences from an English-Japanese comparable corpus. They identify similar article pairs, and then, treating these pairs as parallel texts, align their sentences on a sentence pair similarity score and use DP to find the least-cost alignment over the document pair. Fung and Cheung (2004) approach the problem by using a cosine similarity measure to match foreign and English documents. They work on "very non-parallel corpora". They then generate all possible sentence pairs and select the best ones based on a threshold on cosine similarity scores. Using the extracted sentences they learn a dictionary and iterate over with more sentence pairs. Recent work by Munteanu and Marcu (2005) uses a bilingual lexicon to translate some of the words of the source sentence. These translations are then used to query the database to find matching translations using information retrieval (IR) techniques. Candidate sentences are determined based on word overlap and the decision whether a sentence pair is parallel or not is performed by a maximum entropy classifier trained on parallel sentences. Bootstrapping is used and the size of the learned bilingual dictionary is increased over iterations to get better results.

Our technique is similar to that of (Munteanu and Marcu, 2005) but we bypass the need of the bilingual dictionary by using proper SMT translations and instead of a maximum entropy classifier we use simple measures like the word error rate (WER) and the translation edit rate (TER) to decide whether sentences are parallel or not. We also report an extension of our work (Rauf and Schwenk, 2009) by experimenting with an additional filter TERp, and building a named entity noun dictionary using the unknown words from the SMT (section 5.2). TERp has been tried encouraged by the outperformance of TER in our previous study on French-English. We have applied our technique on a different language pair Arabic-English, versus French-English that we reported the technique earlier on. Our use of full SMT sentences, gives us an added advantage of being able to detect one of the major errors of these approaches, also identified by (Munteanu and Marcu, 2005), i.e, the cases where the initial sentences are identical but the retrieved sentence has a tail of extra words at sentence end. We discuss this problem as detailed in section 5.1.

We apply our technique to create a parallel corpus for the Arabic/English language pair. We show that we achieve significant improvements in the BLEU score by adding our extracted corpus to the already available human-translated corpora. We also perform a comparison of the data extracted by our approach and that by (Munteanu and Marcu, 2005) and report the results in Section 5.3.

This paper is organized as follows. In the next section we first describe the baseline SMT system trained on human-provided translations only. We then proceed by explaining our parallel sentence selection scheme and the post-processing. Section 5 summarizes our experimental results and the paper concludes with a discussion and perspectives of this work.

2 Task Description

In this paper, we consider the translation from Arabic into English, under the same conditions as the official NIST 2008 evaluation. The used bitexts include various news wire translations[1] as well as some texts from the GALE project.[2] We also added the 2002 to 2005 test data to the parallel training data (using all reference translations). This corresponds to a total of about 8M Arabic words. Our baseline system is trained on these bitexts only.

We use the 2006 NIST test data as development data and the official NIST 2008 test data as internal test set. All case sensitive BLEU scores are calculated with the NIST scoring tool with respect to four reference translations. Both data sets include texts from news wires as well as newsgroups.

LDC provides large collections of monolingual data, namely the LDC Arabic and English Gigaword corpora. There are two text sources that do exist in Arabic and English: the AFP and XIN collection. It is likely that each corpora contains sentences which are translations of the other. We aim to extract those. We have used the XIN corpus for all of our reported results and the collection of the AFP and XIN for comparison with ISI. Table 1 summarizes the characteristics of the corpora used. Note that the English part is much larger than the Arabic one (we found the same to be the case for French-English AFP comparable corpora that we used in our previous study). The number of words are given after tokenization.

Source	Arabic	English
AFP	138M	527M
XIN	51M	140M

Table 1: Characteristics of the available comparable Gigaword corpora for the Arabic-English task (number of words).

3 Baseline SMT system

The goal of statistical machine translation (SMT) is to produce a target sentence $\mathbf{e}$ from a source sentence $\mathbf{f}$. It is today common practice to use phrases as translation units (Koehn et al., 2003; Och and Ney, 2003) and a log linear framework in order to introduce several models explaining the translation process:

$$\mathbf{e}^* = \arg\max p(\mathbf{e}|\mathbf{f})$$
$$= \arg\max_e \{exp(\sum_i \lambda_i h_i(\mathbf{e},\mathbf{f}))\} \quad (1)$$

The feature functions h_i are the system models and the λ_i weights are typically optimized to maximize a scoring function on a development set (Och and Ney, 2002). In our system fourteen features functions were used, namely phrase and lexical translation probabilities in both directions, seven features for the lexicalized distortion model, a word and a phrase penalty and a target language model (LM).

The system is based on the Moses SMT toolkit (Koehn et al., 2007) and constructed as follows. First, Giza++ is used to perform word alignments in both directions. Second, phrases and lexical reorderings are extracted using the default settings of the Moses SMT toolkit. The target 4-gram back-off language model is trained on the English part of all bitexts as well as the whole English Gigaword corpus.

4 System Architecture

The general architecture of our parallel sentence extraction system is shown in figure 1. Starting from comparable corpora for the two languages, Arabic and English, we first translate Arabic to English using an SMT system as described in the above sections. These translated texts are then used to perform information retrieval from the English corpus, followed by simple metrics like WER, TER or TERp to filter out good sentence pairs and eventually generate a parallel corpus. We show that a parallel corpus obtained using this technique helps considerably to improve an SMT system.

4.1 System for Extracting Parallel Sentences from Comparable Corpora

We start by translating the Arabic XIN and AFP texts to English using the SMT systems discussed in section 2. In our experiments we considered only the most recent texts (2001-2006, 1.7M sentences; about 65.M Arabic words for XIN). For our experiments on effect on SMT quality we use only the XIN corpus. We use the combination of AFP and XIN for comparison of sentences extracted by our approach with that of (Munteanu and Marcu, 2005). These translations are then treated as queries for the IR process. The design of our sentence extraction process is based on the heuristic that considering the corpus at hand, we

[1] LDC2003T07, 2004E72, T17, T18, 2005E46 and 2006E25.

[2] LDC2005E83, 2006E24, E34, E85 and E92.

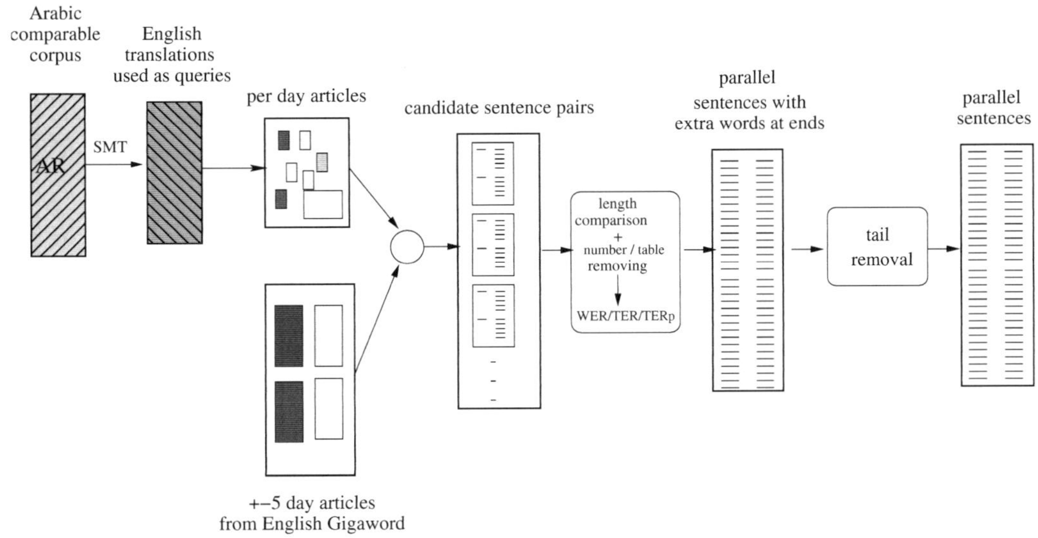

Figure 1: Architecture of the parallel sentence extraction system.

can safely say that a news item reported on day X in the Arabic corpus will be most probably found in the day X-5 and day X+5 time period. We experimented with several window sizes and found the window size of is to be the most accurate in terms of time and the quality of the retrieved sentences. (Munteanu and Marcu, 2005) have also worked with a ± 5 day window.

Using the ID and date information for each sentence of both corpora, we first collect all sentences from the SMT translations corresponding to the same day (query sentences) and then the corresponding articles from the English Gigaword corpus (search space for IR). These day-specific files are then used for information retrieval using a robust information retrieval system. The Lemur IR toolkit (Ogilvie and Callan, 2001) was used for sentence extraction.

The information retrieval step is the most time consuming task in the whole system. The time taken depends upon various factors like size of the index to search in, length of the query sentence etc. To give a time estimate, using a ± 5 day window required 9 seconds per query vs 15 seconds per query when a ± 7 day window was used. We placed a limit of approximately 90 words on the queries and the indexed sentences. This choice was motivated by the fact that the word alignment toolkit Giza++ does not process longer sentences.

A Krovetz stemmer was used while building the index as provided by the toolkit. English stop words, i.e. frequently used words, such as "a" or "the", are normally not indexed because they are so common that they are not useful to query on. The stop word list provided by the IR Group of University of Glasgow[3] was used.

The resources required by our system are minimal : translations of one side of the comparable corpus. It has already been demonstrated in (Rauf and Schwenk, 2009) that when using translations as queries, the quality of the initial SMT is not a factor for better sentence retrieval and that an SMT system trained on small amounts of human-translated data can 'retrieve' potentially good parallel sentences.

4.2 Candidate Sentence Pair Selection

The information retrieval process gives us the potential parallel sentences per query sentence, the decision of their being parallel or not needs to be made about them. At this stage we choose the best scoring sentence as determined by the toolkit and pass the sentence pair through further filters. Gale and Church (1993) based their align program on the fact that longer sentences in one language tend to be translated into longer sentences in the other language, and that shorter sentences tend to be translated into shorter sentences. We initially used the same logic in our selection of the candidate sentence pairs. However our observation was that the filters that we use, WER, TER and TERp implicitly place a penalty when the length differ-

[3] `http://ir.dcs.gla.ac.uk/resources/linguistic_utils/stop_words`

ence between two sentences is too large. Thus using this inherent property, we did not apply any explicit sentence length filtering.

The candidate sentences pairs are then judged based on simple filters. Our choice of filters in accordance to the task in consideration were the WER (Levenshtein distance), Translation Edit Rate (TER) and the relatively new Translation Edit Rate plus (TERp). WER measures the number of operations required to transform one sentence into the other (insertions, deletions and substitutions). A zero WER would mean the two sentences are identical, subsequently lower WER sentence pairs would be sharing most of the common words. However two correct translations may differ in the order in which the words appear, something that WER is incapable of taking into account. This shortcoming is addressed by TER which allows block movements of words and thus takes into account the reorderings of words and phrases in translation (Snover et al., 2006). TERp is an extension of Translation Edit Rate and was one of the top performing metrics at the NIST Metric MATR workshop [4]. It had the highest absolute correlation, as measured by the Pearson correlation coefficient, with human judgments in 9 of the 45 test conditions. TERp tries to address the weaknesses of TER through the use of paraphrases, morphological stemming, and synonyms, as well as edit costs that are optimized to correlate better with various types of human judgments (Snover et al., 2009). The TER filter allows shifts if the two strings (the word sequence in the translated and the IR retrieved sentence) match exactly, however TERp allows shifts if the words being shifted are exactly the same, are synonyms, stems or paraphrases of each other, or any such combination. This allows better sentence comparison by incorporation of sort of linguistic information about words.

5 Experimental evaluation

Our main goal was to be able to create an additional parallel corpus to improve machine translation quality, especially for the domains where we have less or no parallel data available. In this section we report the results of adding these extracted parallel sentences to the already available human-translated parallel sentences.

[4]http://www.itl.nist.gov/iad/mig//tests/metricsmatr/2008/

Bitexts	#words Arabic	BLEU Eval06	BLEU Eval08
Baseline	5.8M	42.64	39.35
+WER-10	5.8M	42.73	39.70
+WER-40	7.2M	43.34	40.59
+WER-60	14.5M	43.95	41.20
+WER-70	20.4M	43.58	41.18
+TER-30	6.5M	43.41	40.08
+TER-50	12.5M	43.90	41.45
+TER-60	17.3M	**44.30**	**41.73**
+TER-75	24.1M	43.79	41.21
+TERp-10	5.8M	42.69	39.80
+TERp-40	10.2M	43.89	41.44
+TERp-60	20.8M	43.94	41.25
+TERp-80	27.7M	43.90	41.58

Table 2: Summary of BLEU scores for the best systems selected based on various thresholds of WER, TER and TERp filters

We conducted a range of experiments by adding our extracted corpus to various combinations of already available human-translated parallel corpora. For our experiments on effect on SMT quality we use only the XIN extracted corpus. We experimented with WER, TER and TERp as filters to select the best scoring sentences. Table 2 shows some of the scores obtained based on BLEU scores on the Dev and test data as a function of the size of the added extracted corpus. The name of the bitext indicates the filter threshold used, for example, TER-50 means sentences selected based on TER filter threshold of 50. Generally, sentences selected based on TER filter showed better BLEU scores on NIST06 than their WER and TERp counter parts up to almost 21M words. Also for the same filter threshold TERp selected longer sentences, followed by TER and then WER, this fact is evident from table 2, where for the filter threshold of 60, TERp and TER select 20.8M and 17.3 words respectively, whereas WER selects 14.5M words.

Figure 2 shows the trend obtained in function of the number of words added. These experiments were performed by adding our extracted sentences to only 5.8M words of human-provided translations. Our best results are obtained when 11.5M of our extracted parallel sentences based on TER filter are added to 5.8M of News wire and gale parallel corpora. We gain an improvement of 1.66 BLEU points on NIST06 and 2.38 BLEU points

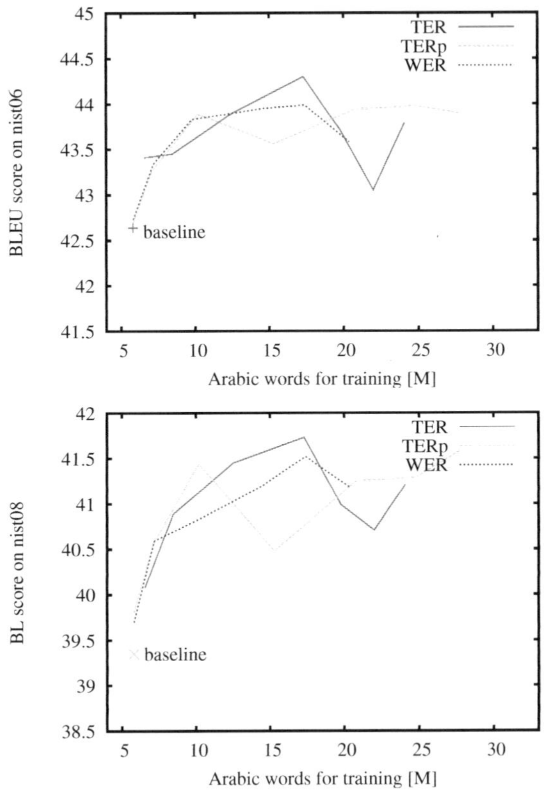

Figure 2: BLEU scores on the NIST06 (Dev, top) and NIST08 (test, bottom) data using an WER,TER or TERp filter as a function of the number of extracted Arabic words added.

on NIST08 (TER-60 in table 2).

An interesting thing to notice in figure 2 is that no filter was able to clearly outperform the others, which is contradictory to our experiments with the French-English language pair (Rauf and Schwenk, 2009), where the TER filter clearly outperformed the WER filter. WER is worse than TER but less evident here than for our previous experiments for the French-English language pair. This performance gain by using the TER filter for French-English was our main motivation for trying TERp. We expected TERp to get better results compared to WER and TER, but TER filter seems the better one among the three filters. Note that all conditions in all the experiments were identical. This gives a strong hint of language pair dependency, making the decision of suitability of a particular filter dependent on the language pair in consideration.

5.1 Sentence tail removal

Two main classes of errors are known when extracting parallel sentences from comparable corpora: firstly, cases where the two sentences share many common words but actually convey different meaning, and secondly, cases where the two sentences are (exactly) parallel except at sentence ends where one sentence has more information than the other. This second case of errors can be detected using WER as we have the advantage of having both the sentences in English. We detected the extra insertions at the end of the IR result sentence and removed them. Some examples of such sentences along with tails detected and removed are shown in figure 3. Since this gives significant improvement in the SMT scores we used it for all our extracted sentences (Rauf and Schwenk, 2009). However, similar to our observations in the last section, the tails were much shorter as compared to our previous experiments with French-English, also most of the tails in this Arabic-English data were of type as shown in last line figure 3. This is a factor dependent on reporting agency and its scheme for reporting, i.e, whether it reports an event independently in each language or uses the translation from one language to the other .

5.2 Dictionary Creation

In our translations, we keep the unknown words as they are, i.e. in Arabic (normally a flag is used so that Moses skips them). This enables us to build a dictionary. Consider the case with translation with one unknown word in Arabic, if all the other words around align well with the English sentence that we found with IR, we could conclude the translation of the unknown Arabic word, see figure 3 line 5. We were able to make a dictionary using this scheme which was comprised mostly of proper nouns often not found in Arabic-English dictionaries. Our proper noun dictionary comprises of about 244K words, some sample words are shown in figure 4. Adding the proper nouns found by this technique to the initial SMT system should help improve translations for new sentences, as these words were before unknown to the system. However, the impact of addition of these words on translation quality is to be evaluated at the moment.

Arabic: بدا الاف الموظفين فى فرز الاصوات التى تم تسجيلها فى عشرات الاف الماكينات الالك ترونية فى 855 بلدة ومدينة عبر البلاد فى الساعة الثامنة صباحا .
Query: *Thousands of officials began counting the votes registered in tens of thousands of electronic machines in 855 towns and cities across the country at 8 a.m.*
Result: *Thousands of officials began counting the votes registered in tens of thousands of electronic machines in 855 towns and cities across the country at 8 a.m.* ***thursday***.
Arabic: كان ويكرمسنغ يشير بذلك الى الجمود الحالى بين حكومته ومتمردى جبهة نمور تحرير ايلام التاميلية .
Query: ويكرمسنغ*was referring to the current stalemate between his government and the Liberation Tigers of Tamil Eelam .*
Result: *Wickremesinghe was referring to the current stalemate between his government and the Liberation Tigers of Tamil Eelam* ***(LTTE) REBELS .***
Arabic: اتخذ بونو هذا الموقف بعد ان طالب بعض المشرعين الحكومة باعادة التفكير فى التواجد العسكرى الاسبانى فى افغانستان .
Query: *Bono adopted this position after some legislators asked the government to rethink the Spanish military presence in Afghanistan .*
Result: *Bono adopted this attitude after some legislators asked the government to reconsider the Spanish military presence in Afghanistan .* ***(SPAIN-AFGHANISTAN) .***

Figure 3: Some examples of an Arabic source sentence, the SMT translation used as query and the potential parallel sentence as determined by information retrieval. Bold parts are the extra tails at the end of the sentences which we automatically removed.

English word from SMT	Arabic unknown word
PetroChina	بتروتشاينا
Bolotine	بولوتين
Amrozi	امروزى
Bulldozers	البولدوزورات
Schulte	شولتى
Jiuxuan	جيوشيوان
Dijmarescu	ديجماريسكو
Aliasghar Soltanieh	اليسجار سلطانيه

Figure 4: Examples of some words found by our dictionary building technique.

5.3 Comparison with previous work

LDC provides extracted parallel texts extracted with the algorithm published by (Munteanu and Marcu, 2005). This corpus contains 1.1M sentence pairs (about 35M words) which were automatically extracted and aligned from the monolingual Arabic and English Gigaword corpora, a confidence score being provided for each sentence pair. We also applied our approach on data provided by LDC, but on a different subset. Since we had used the recent data sets our corpora were till year 2006, whereas ISI's data were till year 2004. We filtered our data according to the time interval of their data (date information was provided for each sentence pair) and used them to compare the two data sets. Both AFP and XIN were used in these comparison experiments since the available ISI's data was comprised of these two collections.

To perform the comparison, we have, firstly, the ISI parallel sentences and secondly the parallel sentences extracted by using our approach using the same time frame and comparable corpora as ISI. We used our sentences as filtered by the TER filter and added them to the already available 5.8M of human-translated (as done in previous experiments). The result is shown graphically in figure 5. Adding the ISI parallel data to the 5.8M baseline parallel corpus (total 27.5M words) yielded a BLEU score of 43.59 on NIST06 Dev set and 41.84 BLEU points on NIST08 test set. Whereas we were able to achieve a BLEU score of 43.88 on NIST06 Dev and 41.35 on NIST08 test set (using a total of 16.1M words), which amounts to an increase of 0.29 BLEU points on the NIST06 Dev set. Note that this gain is achieved by using a total of only 10.3M of our extracted words as compared to 21.7M of ISI corpus to get their best result. However we were not able to improve as much on the NIST08 test corpus.

The trend in BLEU score in figure 5 clearly

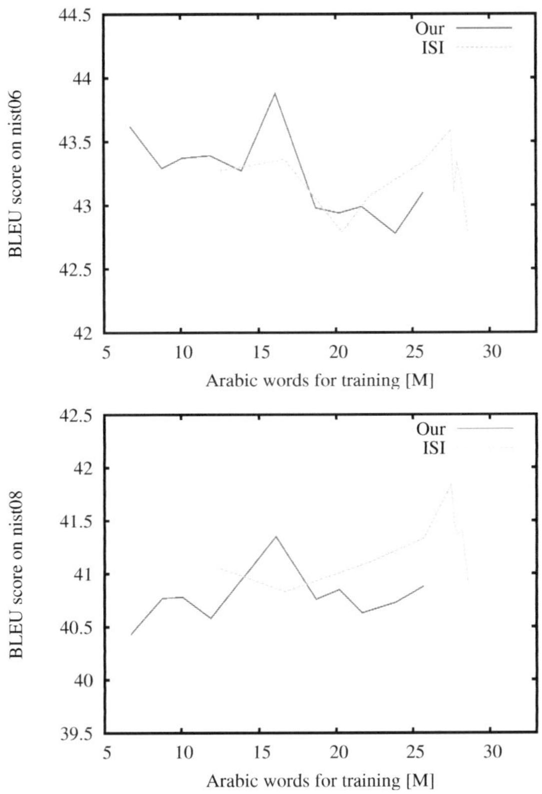

Figure 5: BLEU scores on the NIST06 and NIST08 data using the ISI parallel corpus and our comparative extracted bitexts in function of number of extracted Arabic words added.

shows that our sentence selection scheme selects good sentences, and is capable of achieving the same scores but with much less sentences. This is because in the scheme of ISI, the confidence scores provided are based on the IR and maximum entropy classifier scoring scheme, whereas our filters score the sentences based on linguistic sentence similarity, allowing us to retrieve the good sentence pairs from the bad ones. Once information retrieval is done, which is the most time consuming task in both the techniques, our approach is better able to sort out the good IR extracted sentences as is evident from the results obtained. Moreover our scheme does not require any complex operations, just simple filters which are well adapted to the problem at hand.

6 Conclusion and discussion

Sentence-aligned bilingual texts are a crucial resource to build SMT systems. For some language pairs bilingual corpora just do not exist, the existing corpora are too small to build a good SMT system or they are not of the same genre or domain. This need for parallel corpora, has made the researchers employ new techniques and methods in an attempt to reduce the dire need of this crucial resource of the SMT systems. Our study also contributes in this regard by employing an SMT itself and information retrieval techniques to produce additional parallel corpora from easily available comparable corpora.

We use translations of the source language comparable corpus to find the corresponding parallel sentences from the target language comparable corpus. We only used a limited amount of human-provided bilingual resources. Starting with small amounts of sentence aligned bilingual data large amounts of monolingual data are translated. These translations are then employed to find the corresponding matching sentences in the target side corpus, using information retrieval methods. Simple filters are used to determine whether the retrieved sentences are parallel or not. By adding these retrieved parallel sentences to already available human translated parallel corpora we were able to improve the BLEU score on the test set(NIST08) by 2.38 points for the Arabic-English language pair.

Contrary to the previous approaches as in (Munteanu and Marcu, 2005) which used small amounts of in-domain parallel corpus as an initial resource, our system exploits the target language side of the comparable corpus to attain the same goal, thus the comparable corpus itself helps to better extract possible parallel sentences. We have also presented a comparison with their approach and found our bitexts to achieve nice improvements using much less words. The LDC comparable corpora were used in this paper, but the same approach can be extended to extract parallel sentences from huge amounts of corpora available on the web by identifying comparable articles using techniques such as (Yang and Li, 2003) and (Resnik and Y, 2003).We have successfully applied our approach to French-English and Arabic-English language pairs. As this study strongly hinted towards language pair dependancy on the choice of the filter to use to select better sentences, we intend to investigate this trend in detail.

References

Pascale Fung and Percy Cheung. 2004. Mining very-non-parallel corpora: Parallel sentence and lexicon extraction via bootstrapping and em. In Dekang Lin and Dekai Wu, editors, *EMNLP*, pages 57–63, Barcelona, Spain, July. Association for Computational Linguistics.

William A. Gale and Kenneth W. Church. 1993. A program for aligning sentences in bilingual corpora. *Computational Linguistics*, 19(1):75–102.

Hiroyuki Kaji. 2003. Word sense acquisition from bilingual comparable corpora. In *NAACL '03: Proceedings of the 2003 Conference of the North American Chapter of the Association for Computational Linguistics on Human Language Technology*, pages 32–39, Morristown, NJ, USA. Association for Computational Linguistics.

Philipp Koehn, Franz Josef Och, and Daniel Marcu. 2003. Statistical phrased-based machine translation. In *HLT/NACL*, pages 127–133.

Philipp Koehn et al. 2007. Moses: Open source toolkit for statistical machine translation. In *ACL, demonstration session*.

Dragos Stefan Munteanu and Daniel Marcu. 2005. Improving machine translation performance by exploiting non-parallel corpora. *Computational Linguistics*, 31(4):477–504.

Douglas W. Oard. 1997. Alternative approaches for cross-language text retrieval. In *In AAAI Symposium on Cross-Language Text and Speech Retrieval. American Association for Artificial Intelligence*.

Franz Josef Och and Hermann Ney. 2002. Discriminative training and maximum entropy models for statistical machine translation. In *ACL*, pages 295–302.

Franz Josef Och and Hermann Ney. 2003. A systematic comparison of various statistical alignement models. *Computational Linguistics*, 29(1):19–51.

Paul Ogilvie and Jamie Callan. 2001. Experiments using the Lemur toolkit. In *In Proceedings of the Tenth Text Retrieval Conference (TREC-10)*, pages 103–108.

Reinhard Rapp. 1995. Identifying word translations in non-parallel texts. In *Proceedings of the 33rd annual meeting on Association for Computational Linguistics*, pages 320–322, Morristown, NJ, USA. Association for Computational Linguistics.

Sadaf Abdul Rauf and Holger Schwenk. 2009. On the use of comparable corpora to improve SMT performance. In *EACL*, pages 16–23.

Philip Resnik and Noah A. Smith Y. 2003. The web as a parallel corpus. *Computational Linguistics*, 29:349–380.

Matthew Snover, Bonnie Dorr, Richard Schwartz, Linnea Micciulla, and John Makhoul. 2006. A study of translation edit rate with targeted human annotation. In *ACL*.

Matthew Snover, Bonnie Dorr, and Richard Schwartz. 2008. Language and translation model adaptation using comparable corpora. In *Proceedings of the 2008 Conference on Empirical Methods in Natural Language Processing*, pages 857–866, Honolulu, Hawaii, October. Association for Computational Linguistics.

Matthew Snover, Nitin Madnani, Bonnie Dorr, and Richard Schwartz. 2009. Fluency, adequacy, or HTER? Exploring different human judgments with a tunable MT metric. In *Proceedings of the Fourth Workshop on Statistical Machine Translation*, pages 259–268, Athens, Greece, March. Association for Computational Linguistics.

Richard Sproat, Tao Tao, and ChengXiang Zhai. 2006. Named entity transliteration with comparable corpora. In *ACL-44: Proceedings of the 21st International Conference on Computational Linguistics and the 44th annual meeting of the Association for Computational Linguistics*, pages 73–80, Morristown, NJ, USA. Association for Computational Linguistics.

Masao Utiyama and Hitoshi Isahara. 2003. Reliable measures for aligning Japanese-English news articles and sentences. In Erhard Hinrichs and Dan Roth, editors, *ACL*, pages 72–79.

Christopher C. Yang and Kar Wing Li. 2003. Automatic construction of English/Chinese parallel corpora. *J. Am. Soc. Inf. Sci. Technol.*, 54(8):730–742.

Compilation of Specialized Comparable Corpora in French and Japanese

Lorraine Goeuriot, Emmanuel Morin and Béatrice Daille
LINA - Université de Nantes
France
firstname.lastname@univ-nantes.fr

Abstract

We present in this paper the development of a specialized comparable corpora compilation tool, for which quality would be close to a manually compiled corpus. The comparability is based on three levels: domain, topic and type of discourse. Domain and topic can be filtered with the keywords used through web search. But the detection of the type of discourse needs a wide linguistic analysis. The first step of our work is to automate the detection of the type of discourse that can be found in a scientific domain (science and popular science) in French and Japanese languages. First, a contrastive stylistic analysis of the two types of discourse is done on both languages. This analysis leads to the creation of a reusable, generic and robust typology. Machine learning algorithms are then applied to the typology, using shallow parsing. We obtain good results, with an average precision of 80% and an average recall of 70% that demonstrate the efficiency of this typology. This classification tool is then inserted in a corpus compilation tool which is a text collection treatment chain realized through IBM UIMA system. Starting from two specialized web documents collection in French and Japanese, this tool creates the corresponding corpus.

1 Introduction

Comparable corpora are sets of texts in different languages, that are not translations, but share some characteristics (Bowker and Pearson, 2002). They represent useful resources from which are extracted multilingual terminologies (Déjean et al., 2002) or multilingual lexicons (Fung and Yee, 1998). Comparable corpora are also used in contrastive multilingual studies framework (Peters and Picchi, 1997), they constitute a precious resource for translators (Laviosa, 1998) and teachers (Zanettin, 1998), as they provide a way to observe languages in use.

Their compilation is easier than parallel corpora compilation, because translated resources are rare and there is a lack of resources when the languages involved do not include English. Furthermore, the amount of multilingual documents available on the Web ensures the possibility of automatically compiling them. Nevertheless, this task can not be summarized to a simple collection of documents sharing vocabulary. It is necessary to respect the common characteristics of texts in corpora, established before the compilation, according to the corpus finality (McEnery and Xiao, 2007). Many works are about compilation of corpora from the Web (Baroni and Kilgarriff, 2006) but none, in our knowledge, focuses on compilation of comparable corpora, which has to satisfy many constraints. We fix three comparability levels: domain, topic and type of discourse. Our goal is to automate recognition of these comparability levels in documents, in order to include them into a corpus. We work on Web documents on specialized scientific domains in French and Japanese languages. As document topics can be filtered with keywords in the Web search (Chakrabarti et al., 1999), we focus in this paper on automatic recognition of types of discourse that can be found in scientific documents: science and popular science. This classification tool is then inserted in a specialized comparable corpora compilation tool, which is developped through the Unstructured Information Man-

Proceedings of the 2nd Workshop on Building and Using Comparable Corpora, ACL-IJCNLP 2009, pages 55–63,
Suntec, Singapore, 6 August 2009. ©2009 ACL and AFNLP

agement Architecture (UIMA) (Ferrucci and Lally, 2004).

This paper is structured as follows. After an introduction of related works in section 2, stylistic analysis of our corpus will be presented in section 3. This analysis will lead to the creation of a typology of scientific and popular science discourse type in specifialized domains. The application of learning algorithms to the typology will be described in section 4, and the results will be presented in section 5. We will show that our typology, based on linguistically motivated features, can characterize science and popular science discourses in French and Japanese documents, and that the use of our three comparablility levels can improve corpora comparability. Finally, we describe the development of the corpus compilation tool.

2 Background

"A comparable corpus can be defined as a corpus containing components that are collected using the same sampling frame and similar balance and representativeness" (McEnery and Xiao, 2007, p. 20). Comparability is ensured using characteristics which can refer to the text creation context (period, author...), or to the text itself (topic, genre...). The choice of the common characteristics, which define the content of corpora, affects the *degree of comparability*, notion used to quantify how two corpora can be comparable. The choice of these characteristics depends on the finality of the corpus. Among papers on comparable corpora, we distinguish two types of works, which induces different choices:

- General language works, where texts of corpora usually share a domain and a period. Fung and Yee (1998) used a corpus composed of newspaper in English and Chinese on a specific period to extract words translations, using IR and NLP methods. Rapp (1999) used a English / German corpus, composed of documents coming from newspapers as well as scientific papers to study alignment methods and bilingual lexicon extraction from non-parallel corpora (which can be considered as comparable);
- Specialized language works, where choice of criteria is various. Déjean et al. (2002) used a corpus composed of scientific abstracts from *Medline*, a medical portal, in English and German. Thus they used documents sharing a domain and a genre to extract bilingual terminology. Chiao (2002) used a corpus of documents of medical domain on a specific topic to work on the extraction of specialized terminologies.

In general language works, documents of comparable corpora often share characteristics like domain or topic. As they are usually extracted from newspapers, it is important to limit them to a certain period to guarantee their comparability.

In specialized corpora, first levels of comparability can be achieved with the domain and the topic. Moreover, several communicative settings appear in specialized language (Bowker and Pearson, 2002): expert-expert, expert-initiate, relative expert to the uninitiated, teacher-pupil. Malrieu and Rastier (2002) specify several levels of textual classification, each of which corresponding to a certain granularity. The first level is *discourse*, defined as a set of utterances from a enunciator characterized by a global topical unit (Ducrot and Todorov, 1972). The second level is *genre*, defined as text categories distinguished by matured speakers. For example, to literary discourse correspond several genres: drama, poetry, prose... Inspired by these communicative settings and textual categories, we choose to distinguish two communicative settings or *type of discourse* in specialized domains: science (texts written by experts to experts) and popular science (texts written to non-experts, by experts, semi-experts or non-experts). This comparability level, the type of discourse, reflects the context of production or usage of the documents, and guarantees a lexical homogeneity in corpora (Bowker and Pearson, 2002, p. 27). Furthermore, Morin et al. (2007) proved that comparable corpora sharing a topic and a type of discourse are well adapted for multilingual terminologies extraction.

Our goal is to create a tool to compile comparable corpora in French and Japanese which documents are extracted from the Web. We investigate automatic categorization of documents according to their type of discourse. This categorization is based on a typology of elements characterizing these types of discourse. To this end, we carry out a stylistic and contrastive analysis (Karlgren, 1998). This analysis aims to highlight linguistically motivated features through several dimensions (structural, modal and lexical), whose combination characterizes scientific or popular science discourse. A specialized comparable corpus can be compiled from a single type of discourse document collection through several steps. Last part of this paper focuses on the automation of these steps using the IBM Unstructured Information Management Architecture (`UIMA`).

3 Analysis of Types of Discourse

The recognition of types of discourse is based on a stylistic analysis adapted from a deductive and contrastive method, which purpose is to raise discriminant and linguistically motivated features characterizing these two types of discourse. Main difficulty here is to find relevant features which fit every language involved. These features, gathered in a typology, will be used to adapt machine learning algorithms to compilation of corpora. This typology thus needs to be robust, generic and reusable in other languages and domains. Genericity is ensured by a broad typology composed of features covering a wide range of documents characteristics, while robustness is guaranteed with operational (computable) features and treatment adaptable to Web documents as well as texts.

Sinclair (1996) distinguishes two levels of analysis in his report on text typologies: external level, characterizing the context of creation of the document; and internal level, corresponding to linguistic characteristics of document. Because our corpora are composed of documents extracted from the Web, we consider external level features as all the features related to the creation of documents and their structure (non-linguistic features) and call them *structural features*. Stylistic analysis raises several granularity levels among linguistic characteristics of the texts. We thus distinguish two levels in the internal dimension. Firstly, in order to distinguish between scientific and popular science documents, we need to consider the speaker in his speech: the modality. Secondly, scientific discourse can be characterized by vocabulary, word length and other lexical features. Therefore our typology is based on three analysis levels: structural, modal and lexical.

3.1 Structural Dimension

When documents are extracted from the Web, the structure and the context of creation of the documents should be considered. In the framework of Web documents classification, several elements bring useful information: pictures, videos and other multimedia contents (Asirvatham and Ravi, 2001); meta-information, title and *HTML* structure (Riboni, 2002). While those information are not often used in comparable corpora, they can be used to classify them. Table 1 shows structural features.

Feature	French	Japanese
URL pattern	×	
Document's format	×	×
Meta tags	×	×
Title tag	×	×
Pages layout	×	×
Pages background	×	×
Images	×	×
Links	×	×
Paragraphs	×	×
Item lists	×	×
Number of sentences	×	×
Typography	×	×
Document's length	×	×

Table 1: Structural dimension features

3.2 Modal Dimension

The degree of specialization required by the recipient or reader is characterized by the relation built in the utterance between the speaker or author and the recipient or reader[1]. The tone and linguistic elements in texts define this relation. The modalisation is an interpretation of the author's attitude toward the content of his/her assertion. Modalisation is characterized by many textual markers: verbs, adverbs, politeness forms, etc. Presence of the speaker and his position towards his speech are quite different in scientific and popular science discourse. Thus we think modalisation markers can be relevant. For example, the speaker directly speaks to the reader in some popular science documents: "*By eating well, you'll also help to prevent diabetes problems that can occur later in life, like heart disease*". Whereas a scientific document would have a neutral tone: "*Obesity plays a central role in the insulin resistance syndrome, which includes hyperinsulinemia, [...] and an increased risk of atherosclerotic cardiovascular disease*".

Most of the modal theories are language dependent, and use description phenomena that are specific to each language. Conversely, the theory exposed in (Charaudeau, 1992) is rather indepen-

[1] Since we work on a scientific domain, we will consider the speaker as the author of texts, and the recipient as the reader.

dent of the language and operational for French and Japanese (Ishimaru, 2006). According to Charaudeau (1992, p.572), modalisation clarifies the position of the speaker with respect to his reader, to himself and to his speech. Modalisation is composed of locutive acts, particular positions of the author in his speech, and each locutive act is characterized by modalities. We kept in his theory two locutive acts involving the author:

Allocutive act: the author gets the reader involved in the speech (ex.: "*You have to do this.*");

Elocutive act: the author is involved in his own speech, he reveals his position regarding his speech (ex.: "*I would like to do this.*").

Each of these acts are then divided into several modalities. These modalities are presented in table 2 with English examples. Some of the modalities are not used in a language or another, because they are not frequent or too ambiguous.

3.3 Lexical Dimension

Biber (1988) uses lexical information to observe variations between texts, especially between genres and types of texts. Karlgren (1998) also use lexical information to characterize text genres, and use them to observe stylistic variations among texts. Thus, we assume that lexical information is relevant in the distinction between science and popular science discourse. Firstly, because a specialized vocabulary is a principal characteristic of specialized domain texts (Bowker and Pearson, 2002, p. 26). Secondly, because scientific documents contain more complex lexical units, nominal compounds or nominal sentences than popular science documents (Sager, 1990).

Table 3 presents the lexical dimension features. Note that these features show a higher language dependency than other dimension features.

Feature	French	Japanese
Specialized vocabulary	×	×
Numerals	×	×
Units of measurement	×	×
Words length	×	
Bibliography	×	×
Bibliographic quotes	×	×
Punctuation	×	×
Sentences end		×
Brackets	×	×
Other alphabets (latin, hiragana, katakana)		×
Symbols		×

Table 3: Lexical dimension features

Dimension	Method
Structural	Pattern matching
Modal	Lexical and lexico-syntactic patterns
Lexical	Lexical patterns

Table 4: Markers detection methods

4 Automatic Classification by Type of Discourse

The process of documents classification can be divided into three steps: document indexing, classifier learning and classifier evaluation (Sebastiani, 2002). Document indexing consists in building a compact representation of documents that can be interpreted by a classifier. In our case, each document d_i is represented as a vector of features weight: $\vec{d_i} = \{w_{1i}, \ldots, w_{ni}\}$ where n is the number of features of the typology and w_{ij} is the weight of the jth feature in the ith document. Each feature weight is normalized, dividing the weight by the total. Documents indexing is characterized by our typology (section 3) and features implementation.

4.1 Features Implementation

In order to get a fast classification system, we privileged for the implementation of our typology features shallow parsing such as lexical markers and lexico-syntactic patterns (method for each dimension is detailed in table 4).

Structural Features We used 12 structural features introduced in section 3.1. Most of these features are achieved through pattern matching. For example, URL patterns can determine is the document belongs to websites such as hospital (`http://www.chu-***.fr`) or universities websites (`http://www.univ-***.fr`), etc. As for paragraphs, images, links, etc., one simple search of `HTML` tags was made.

Modal Features Locutor presence markers in a text can be implicit or ambiguous. We focused here on simple markers of his presence in order to avoid *noise* in our results (high precision but weak recall). Thus we don't recognize all modal markers in a text but those recognized are correct. There are pronouns which are specific to the speech act: for instance, for the elocutive act, the French pronouns *je* (I) and *nous* (we), and the Japanese pronouns 私 (I), 私達 (we)

Feature	Example	French	Japanese
Allocutive modality			
Allocutive personal pronouns	*You*	×	
Injunction modality	*Don't do this*	×	×
Authorization modality	*You can do this*	×	
Judgement modality	*Congratulations for doing it!*	×	
Suggestion modality	*You should do this*	×	×
Interrogation modality	*When do you arrive?*	×	×
Interjection modality	*How are you, Sir?*	×	
Request modality	*Please, do this*	×	×
Elocutive modality			
Elocutive personal	*I, we*	×	×
Noticing modality	*We notice that he left*	×	×
Knowledge modality	*I know that he left*	×	×
Opinion modality	*I think he left*	×	×
Will modality	*I would like him to leave*	×	×
Promise modality	*I promise to be here*	×	×
Declaration modality	*I affirm he left*		×
Appreciation modality	*I like this*	×	
Commitment modality	*We have to do this*	×	
Possibility modality	*I can inform them*	×	

Table 2: Modal dimension features

and 我々 (we). The modalities are also computed with lexical markers. For example, the modality of knowledge can be detected in French with verbs like *savoir, connaître* (know), and in Japanese with the verb 知る (know), with polite form 知っています and with neutral form 知っている.

Lexical Features Some of our lexical criteria are specific to the scientific documents, like bibliographies and bibliographic quotations, specialized vocabulary or the measurement units. To measure the terminological density (proportion of specialized vocabulary in the text) in French, we evaluate terms with stems of Greek-Latin (Namer and Baud, 2007) and suffix characters of relational adjectives that are particularly frequent in scientific domains (Daille, 2000). We listed about 50 stems such as *inter-*, *auto-* or *nano-*, and the 10 relational suffixes such such as *-ique* or *-al*. For Japanese, we listed prefix characteristics of names of disease or symptoms (先天性 (congenital), 遺伝性(hereditary), etc.). These stems can be found in both type of discourse, but not in the same proportions. Specialized terms are used in both type of discourse in different ways. For example, the term "ovarectomie" (*ovarectomy*) can be frequent in a scientific document and used once in a popular science documents to explain it and then replaced by "ablation des ovaires" (*ovary ablation*). Sentences end are specific ending particles used in japanese, for example the particle か is often used at the end of an interrogative sentence.

4.2 Learning Algorithms

Classifier learning is a process which observes features weight of documents classified in a class c or $\overline{c}$ and determine characteristics that a new document should have to be classified in one of these two classes [2]. Given a document indexing, there are some well-known algorithms that can achieve this process (neural network, Bayes classifiers, SVM, etc.) of which Sebastiani (2002) carried out a research about the assemblage and comparison. Applied to a Reuters newswires corpus, these techniques showed variable performances in the usage level of supervised or unsupervised approaches, of the size of the corpus, of the number of categories, etc. We decided to use *SVMlight* (Joachims, 2002) and *C4.5* (Quinlan, 1993), since both of them seem to be the most appropriate to our data (small corpora, binary classification, less than 100 features).

5 Experiments

In this section, we describe the two comparable corpora used and present the two experiments carried out with each of them. The first comparable corpus is used to train the classifier in order to learn a classification model based on our typology (*i.e.* training task). The second comparable corpus is used to evaluate the impact of the classification model when applied on new documents (*i.e.* evaluation task).

[2]This is the binary case. See (Sebastiani, 2002) for other cases.

5.1 Comparable Corpora

The corpora used in our experiments are both composed of French and Japanese documents harvested from the Web. The documents were taken from the medical domain, within the topic of *diabetes and nutrition* for training task, and *breast cancer* for the evaluation task. Document harvesting was carried out with a domain-based search and a manual selection. Documents topic is filtered using keywords reflecting the specialized domain: for example *alimentation*, *diabète* and *obésité* [3] for French part and 糖尿病 and 肥満 [4] for the Japanese part of the training task corpus. Those keywords are directly related to the topic or they can be synonyms (found on thesaurus) or semantically linked terms (found in Web documents collected). Then the documents were manually selected by native speakers of each language who are not domain specialists, and classified with respect to their type of discourse: science (SC) or popular science (PS). Manual classification is based on the following heuristics, to decide their type of discourse:

- A scientific document is written by specialists to specialists.
- We distinguish two levels of popular science: texts written by specialists for the general public and texts written by the general public for the general public. Without distinction of these last two levels, we privileged documents written by specialists, assuming that they may be richer in content and vocabulary (for example advices from a doctor would be richer and longer than forum discussions).

Our manual classification is based on the two previous heuristics, and endorsed by several empirical elements: website's origin, vocabulary used, etc. The classification of ambiguous documents has been validated by linguists. A few documents for which it was difficult to decide on the type of discourse, such as those written by people whose specialist status was not clear, were not retained.

We thus created two comparable corpora:

- [DIAB_CP] related to the topic of *diabetes and nutrition* and used to train the classifier.
- [BC_CP] related to the topic of *breast cancer* and used to evaluate the effectiveness of the classifier.

Table 5 shows the main features of each comparable corpora: the number of documents, and the number of words[5] for each language and each type of discourse.

			# docs	# words
[DIAB_CP]	FR	SC	65	425,781
		PS	183	267,885
	JP	SC	119	234,857
		PS	419	572,430
[BC_CP]	FR	SC	50	443,741
		PS	42	71,980
	JP	SC	48	211,122
		PS	51	123,277

Table 5: Basic data on each comparable corpora

5.2 Results

We present in this section two classification tasks:

- the first one consists in training and testing classifiers with [DIAB_CP], using N-fold cross validation method that consists in dividing the corpus into n sub-samples of the same size (we fix $N = 5$). Results are for 5 partitioning on average;
- the second one consists in testing on [BC_CP] the best classifier learned on [DIAB_CP], in order to evaluate its impact on new documents.

Tables 6 and 7 show results of these two tasks. On both table we present precision and recall metrics with the two learning systems used. On table 6, we can see that the results concerning the French documents are quite satisfactory altogether, with a recall on average of 87%, and a precision on average of 90% as for the classifier *C4.5* (more than 215 documents are well classified from 248 French documents of [DIAB_CP]). The results of the classification in Japanese are also good with the classifier C.4.5. More than 90% of documents are correctly classified, and the precision reaches on average 80%. Some of the lower results can be explained, especially in Japanese by the high range of document genres in the corpus (research papers, newspapers, scientific magazines, recipes, job offers, forum discussions…).

[3] *nutrition*, *diabetes*, and *obesity*

[4] *diabetes* and *overweight*

[5] For Japanese, the number of words is the number of occurrences recognized by ChaSen (Matsumoto et al., 1999)

		French		Japanese	
		Prec.	Rec.	Prec.	Rec.
svml	SC	1.00	0.36	0.70	0.65
	PS	0.80	1,00	0.72	0.80
c4.5	SC	0.89	0.80	0.76	0.96
	PS	0.91	0.94	0.95	0.99

Table 6: Precision and recall for each language, each classifier, on [DIAB_CP]

Table 7 shows results on [BC_CP]. In general, we note a decrease of the results with [BC_CP], although results are still satisfactory. French documents are well classified whatever the classifier is, with a precision higher than 75% and a recall higher than 75%, which represent more than 70 well classified documents on 92. Japanese documents are well classified too, with 76% precision and 77% recall on average, with 23 documents wrong classified on 99. This classification model is effective when it is applied to a different medical topic. This classification model seems efficient to recognize scientific discourse from popular science one in French and Japanese documents on a particular topic.

		French		Japanese	
		Prec.	Rec.	Prec.	Rec.
svml	SC	0.92	0.53	0.90	0.61
	PS	0.64	0.95	0.66	0.98
c4.5	SC	0.70	0.92	0.76	0.70
	PS	0.87	0.56	0.75	0.80

Table 7: Precision and recall for each language, each classifier, on [BC_CP]

6 Comparable Corpora Compilation Tool

Compilation of a corpus, whatever type it is, is composed of several steps.

1. Corpus Specifications: they must be defined by the creator or user of the corpus. It includes decisions on its type, languages involved, resources from which are extracted documents, its size, etc. In the case of specialized comparable corpora, specifications concern languages involved, size, resources and documents domain, theme and type of discourse. This step depends on the applicative goals of the corpus and has to be done carefully.

2. Documents Selection and Collection: according to the resource, size and other corpus criteria chosen during the first step, documents are collected.

3. Documents Normalization and Annotation: cleaning and linguistic treatments are applied to documents in order to convert them into raw texts and annotated texts.

4. Corpus Documentation: compilation of a corpus that can be used in a durable way must include this step. Documentation of the corpus includes information about the compilation (creator, date, method, resources, etc.) and information about the corpus documents. Text Encoding Initiative (TEI) standard has been created in order to conserve in an uniformed way this kind of information in a corpus [6].

A corpus quality highly depends on the first two steps. Moreover, these steps are directly linked to the creator use of the corpus. The first step must be realized by the user to create an relevant corpus. Although second step can be computerizable (Rogelio Nazar and Cabré, 2008), we choose to keep it manual in order to guarantee corpus quality. We decided to work on a system which realizes the last steps, *i.e.* normalization, annotation and documentation, starting from a collection of documents selected by a user.

Our tool has been developed on Unstructured Information Management Architecture (UIMA) that has been created by *IBM Research Division* (Ferrucci and Lally, 2004). Unstructured data (texts, images, etc.) collections can be easily treated on this platform and many libraries are available. Our tool starts with a web documents or texts collection and is composed of several components realizing each part of the creation of the corpus:

1. the collection is loaded and documents are converted to texts (with conversion tools from pdf or html to text mainly);

2. all texts are cleaned and normalized (noise from the conversion is cleaned, all texts are converted into the same encoding, etc.);

[6] http://www.tei-c.org/index.xml

3. a pre-syntactic treatment is applied on texts (segmentation mainly) to prepare them for the following step;

4. morphologic and morpho-syntactic tagging tools are applied on the texts (Brill tagger (Brill, 1994) and Flemm lemmer (Namer, 2000) for French texts, Chasen (Matsumoto et al., 1999) for Japanese);

5. texts are classified according to their type of discourse: we use here the most efficient `SVMlight` classifier. In fact, two corpus are created, on for each type of discourse, then the user can choose one of them. A vectorial representation of each document is computed, then these vectors are classified with the classifier selected.

6. documentation is produced for the corpus, a certain amount of information are included and they can be easily completed by the user.

In reality, this tool is more a compilation assistant than a compilator. It facilitates the compilation task: the user is in charge of the most important part of the compilation, but the technical part (treatment of each document) is realized by the system. This guarantee a high quality in the corpus.

7 Conclusion

This article has described a first attempt of compiling smart comparable corpora. The quality is close to a manually collected corpus, and the high degree of comparability is guaranteed by a common domain and topic, but also by a same type of discourse. In order to detect automatically some of the comparability levels, we carried out a stylistic and contrastive analysis and elaborated a typology for the characterization of scientific and popular science types of discourse on the Web. This typology is based on three aspects of Web documents: the structural aspect, the modal aspect and lexical aspect. From the modality part, this distinction is operational even on linguistically distant languages, as we proved by the validation on French and Japanese. Our typology, implemented using *SVMlight* and *C4.5* learning algorithms brought satisfactory results of classification, not only on the training corpus but also on an evaluation corpus, since we obtained a precision on average of 80% and a recall of 70%. This classifier has then been included into a tool to assist specialized comparable corpora compilation. Starting from a Web documents collection selected by the user, this tool realizes cleaning, normalization and linguistic treatment of each document and "physically" creates the corpus.

This tool is a first attempt and can be improved. In a first time, we would like to assist the selection and collection of documents, which could be realized through the tool. Moreover, we would like to investigate needs of comparable corpora users in order to adapt our tool. Finally, others languages could be added to the system, which represents a quite time-consuming task: a classifier would have to be created so all the linguistic analysis and classification tasks would have to be done again for other languages.

Acknowledgement

This research program has been funded by the French National Research Agency (ANR) through the C-mantic project (ANR-07-MDCO-002-01) 2008-2010. We thank Yukie Nakao for the japanese corpus and linguistic resources.

References

Arul Prakash Asirvatham and Kranthi Kumar Ravi. 2001. Web page classification based on document structure. *IEEE National Convention*.

Marco Baroni and Adam Kilgarriff. 2006. Large linguistically-processed web corpora for multiple languages. In *EACL'06*, pages 87–90. The Association for Computer Linguistics.

Douglas Biber. 1988. *Variation across Speech and Writing*. Cambridge University Press.

Lynne Bowker and Jennifer Pearson. 2002. *Working with Specialized Language: A Practical Guide to Using Corpora*. London/New York, Routeledge.

Eric Brill. 1994. Some advances in transformation-based part of speech tagging. In *Proceedings of the 12th National Conference on Artificial Intelligence (AAAI'94)*, pages 722–727, Seattle, WA, USA.

Soumen Chakrabarti, Martin van den Berg, and Byron Dom. 1999. Focused crawling: a new approach to topic-specific Web resource discovery. *Computer Networks (Amsterdam, Netherlands: 1999)*, 31(11–16):1623–1640.

Patrick Charaudeau. 1992. *Grammaire du sens et de l'expression*. Hachette.

Yun-Chuang Chiao and Pierre Zweigenbaum. 2002. Looking for candidate translational equivalents in specialized, comparable corpora. In *COLING'02*, pages 1208–1212, Tapei, Taiwan.

Béatrice Daille. 2000. Morphological rule induction for terminology acquisition. In *COLING'00*, pages 215–221, Sarrbrucken, Germany.

Hervé Déjean, Éric Gaussier, and Fatia Sadat. 2002. An approach based on multilingual thesauri and model combination for bilingual lexicon extraction. In *COLING'02*.

Oswald Ducrot and Tzvetan Todorov. 1972. *Dictionnaire encyclopédique des sciences du langage*. Éditions du Seuil.

David Ferrucci and Adam Lally. 2004. Uima: An architectural approach to unstructured information processing in the corporate research environment. *Natural Language Engineering*, 10:327–348.

Pascale Fung and Lo Yuen Yee. 1998. An ir approach for translating new words from nonparallel, comparable texts. In Christian Boitet and Pete Whitelock, editors, *COLING'98*, volume 1, pages 414–420, Montreal, Quebec, Canada.

Kumiko Ishimaru. 2006. *Comparative study on the discourse of advertisement in France and Japan: beauty products*. Ph.D. thesis, Osaka University, Japan.

Thorsten Joachims. 2002. *Learning to Classify Text using Support Vector Machines*. Kluwer Academic Publishers.

Jussi Karlgren, 1998. *Natural Language Information Retrieval*, chapter Stylistic Experiments in Information Retrieval. Tomek, Kluwer.

Sarah Laviosa. 1998. Corpus-based approaches to contrastive linguistics and translation studies. *Meta*, 43(4):474–479.

Denise Malrieu and Francois Rastier. 2002. Genres et variations morphosyntaxiques. *Traitement Automatique des Langues (TAL)*, 42(2):548–577.

Yuji Matsumoto, Akira Kitauchi, Tatsuo Yamashita, and Yoshitaka Hirano. 1999. Japanese Morphological Analysis System ChaSen 2.0 Users Manual. Technical report, Nara Institute of Science and Technology (NAIST).

Anthony McEnery and Zhonghua Xiao. 2007. Parallel and comparable corpora: What is happening? In Gunilla Anderman and Margaret Rogers, editors, *Incorporating Corpora: The Linguist and the Translator*. Clevedon: Multilingual Matters.

Fiammetta Namer and Robert Baud. 2007. Defining and relating biomedical terms: Towards a cross-language morphosemantics-based system. *International Journal of Medical Informatics*, 76(2-3):226–233.

Fiametta Namer. 2000. Flemm : Un analyseur flexionnel du français à base de règles. *Traitement Automatique des Langues (TAL)*, 41(2):523–548.

Carol Peters and Eugenio Picchi. 1997. Using linguistic tools and resources in cross-language retrieval. In David Hull and Doug Oard, editors, *Cross-Language Text and Speech Retrieval. Papers from the 1997 AAAI Spring Symposium, Technical Report SS-97-05*, pages 179–188.

J. Ross Quinlan. 1993. *C4.5: Programs for Machine Learning*. Morgan Kaufmann Publishers, San Francisco, CA, USA.

Reinhard Rapp. 1999. Automatic Identification of Word Translations from Unrelated English and German Corpora. In *ACL'99*, pages 519–526, College Park, Maryland, USA.

Daniele Riboni. 2002. Feature selection for web page classification. In Hassan Shafazand and A Min Tjoa, editors, *Proceedings of the 1st EurAsian Conference on Advances in Information and Communication Technology (EURASIA-ICT)*, pages 473–478, Shiraz, Iran. Springer.

Jorge Vivaldi Rogelio Nazar and Teresa Cabré. 2008. A suite to compile and analyze an lsp corpus. In Nicoletta Calzolari, Khalid Choukri, Bente Maegaard, Joseph Mariani, Jan Odjik, Stelios Piperidis, and Daniel Tapias, editors, *Proceedings of the Sixth International Language Resources and Evaluation (LREC'08)*, Marrakech, Morocco, may. European Language Resources Association (ELRA).

J. C. Sager. 1990. *A Pratical Course in Terminology Processing*. John Benjamins, Amsterdam.

Fabrizio Sebastiani. 2002. Machine learning in automated text categorization. *ACM Computing Surveys*, 34(1):1–47.

John Sinclair. 1996. Preliminary recommendations on text typology. Technical report, EAGLES (Expert Advisory Group on Language Engineering Standards).

Federico Zanettin. 1998. Bilingual comparable corpora and the training of translators. *Meta*, 43(4):616–630.

Toward Categorization of Sign Language Corpora

Jérémie Segouat
LIMSI-CNRS / Orsay, France
WebSourd / Toulouse, France
jeremie.segouat@limsi.fr

Annelies Braffort
LIMSI-CNRS / Orsay, France
annelies.braffort@limsi.fr

Abstract

This paper addresses the notion of parallel, noisy parallel and comparable corpora in the sign language research field. As it is quite a new field, the categorization of sign language corpora is not well established, and does not rely on a straightforward basis. Nevertheless, several kinds of corpora are now available and could raise interesting issues, provided that adapted tools and techniques are developed.

1 Introduction

Sign Language (SL) is a visual-gestural language, using the whole upper body articulators (chest, arms, hands, head, face, and gaze) in a simultaneous way. Signs (in some way, equivalent to words in vocal languages) are articulated in the signing space located in front of the signer. This is a natural language, with its own linguistic structures and specificities, used by deaf people to communicate in everyday life. It can be considered that there is one SL for each country, as for vocal languages. One particularity is that there is no written form of SL (Garcia, 2006): corpora take the form of videos, thus specific design and analysis methods have to be used. Therefore, NLP and corpus linguistics definitions may have to be adapted to this research field.

1.1 Brief History of Sign Language Corpora

Research in SL has begun with the creation of notation systems. These systems aim to describe in a written form how SL could be performed. Bébian (1825), a French teacher, wrote a book where he proposed a description of the French Sign Language (LSF) using drawings. This description took into account facial expressions and manual gestures. A major study was conducted by Stokoe (1960) on American SL. The aim was also to describe SL, but this time only focused on manual gestures. These studies were based upon live analyses: no video corpus was created. The researchers had to watch how signers were performing SL, and then write down or draw what they were observing.

In the 1980s, Cuxac (1996) created one of the first video SL corpora for linguistic studies. From the 1990s until now, video SL corpora have been created both to be used in linguistic studies, as listed by Brugman (2003), and for gathering lexicons to create dictionaries[1]. A few years ago, some video SL corpora were designed to serve as the basis for NLP and Image Processing (Neidle, 2000).

1.2 Definitions

Fung (2004) distinguishes four kinds of corpora: parallel ("a sentence-aligned corpus containing bilingual translations of the same document"), noisy parallel ("contain non-aligned sentences that are nevertheless mostly bilingual translations of the same document"), comparable ("contain non-sentence-aligned, non-translated bilingual documents that are topic-aligned"), and very-non-parallel ("contains far more disparate, very-non-parallel bilingual documents that could either be on the same topic (in-topic) or not (off-topic)"). If these definitions are still under discussion in the NLP community, there is no such discussion in the community which studies SLs. Would it be possible to apply such definitions to Sign Languages corpora?

Many corpora are mere dictionaries[2], i.e. they only contain isolated signs and no utterances, just signs, but could be considered as very basic parallel SL corpora. As far as we know, there exists very few noisy parallel SL corpora (see section 2.2), and very few comparable SL corpora (Bungeroth 2008, ECHO project[3]).

[1] http://www.spreadthesign.com/country/gb/
[2] http://www.limsi.fr/Scientifique/iles/Theme5/corpus
[3] http://www.let.ru.nl/sign-lang/echo/

Proceedings of the 2nd Workshop on Building and Using Comparable Corpora, ACL-IJCNLP 2009, pages 64–67,
Suntec, Singapore, 6 August 2009. ©2009 ACL and AFNLP

Because not enough data can be found on the way these corpora have been built and the way they are used, it seems difficult to discuss whether Fung's definitions apply to them. Thus, we present in this paper the corpora we have built (section 2) and explain why they could be considered as parallel, noisy parallel or comparable. Section 3 discusses the use of NLP processes for SL corpora analysis, and section 4 presents prospects on existing or possible SL corpora.

2 LIMSI's Sign Language Corpora

2.1 Parallel Corpora

We are currently building a French Sign Language (LSF)-French dictionary (Segouat 2008) that will be available on the Web. We will provide not only French and LSF translations, but also linguistic descriptions of signs, and a functionality to search for signs from their visual aspects or their linguistic descriptions. This is a mere parallel corpus that will be using to analyze the variety of LSF in France (according to where people live, where they have grown, where they learned LSF, etc.).

We have recently built a corpus related to the railway information domain (Segouat, 2009). The starting point is written French sentences that exactly correspond to the vocal announcements made in railways stations. The goal is to provide information in LSF as it is provided vocally: by coarticulating pieces of utterances. Written French sentences were translated into LSF and filmed, in order to study coarticulation in LSF. We use this corpus to analyze how signs are modified according to their context.

We participate in the DictaSign European project (Efthimiou, 2009) that aims at gathering parallel SL corpora from four countries (Greece, England, Germany, and France). One of its purposes is to study translations between different sign languages (SLs) of these four countries. The welcome page of the website[4] includes presentations of the project in the four different SLs that are each direct translations of the corresponding written texts. As it is a starting project, this corpus has not yet been studied nor considered from a comparability point of view.

2.2 Noisy Parallel Corpora

We have taken part in the creation of the LS-COLIN corpus (Cuxac, 2001). The aim of this project was to design a corpus that could be used by linguists and computer scientists. The methodology was the following: each deaf signer (i.e. a person who performs SL) was explained the protocol. The person had to perform several kinds of stories, on several given themes or elicited by using pictures. For the picture based story, the deaf signer was shown six pictures that draw a line for the story, and then expressed the story in LSF. This corpus could be considered as a noisy parallel one, because the LSF version is a translation of the pictures with addition of details. The linguists have created a noisy parallel version of some parts of LS-COLIN, by providing a transcription with glosses (sign to word translation, without taking into consideration the grammatical structure involved: thus there is a lack of information). All the annotations were made in French text, and were used to analyze the grammatical structure of LSF.

We have participated to the WebSi project (Martin, 2009), which aims at evaluating whether common representations could be designed for gestures performed by speaking and signing persons, allowing bilingual applications to be developed. The first step was a study dedicated to the comparison of deictic gestures, both with multimodal-French and LSF utterances. The corpus consists of answers, by a deaf and a hearing person, to eleven questions eliciting responses with deictic gestures of various kinds. A French/LSF interpreter formulated the questions so that both subjects were in the closest possible interaction conditions. The observed productions were indeed very different. In the deaf person's answers, a more complex structure was observed in deictics, because the deictic function is incorporated into the lexical signs, forming what is called indicating signs. However, common global aspects were observed in both types of productions, which are all constituted by pointing using gaze and manual gestures organized with a given temporal structure.

2.3 Comparable corpora

In the LS-COLIN corpus, each deaf signer had to perform a story on several given themes, for example September 11 tragic events. This can be considered as a synchronous comparable corpus because each signer expressed his own version of the same event. The picture-based stories may also be considered as comparable corpora, because deaf signers were asked to perform the story twice: at the beginning and at the end of the recording. Thus it is the same topic, and the two versions are not translations of one another; but

[4] http://www.dictasign.eu

we are not certain that it can be considered as "non-sentence-aligned" because they both follow picture order. Computer scientists have used LS-COLIN from a comparability point of view, to analyze the visual modality in LSF: they studied torso (Segouat, 2006) and facial (Chételat-Pelé, 2008) movements. These studies were made on same-topic stories performed by different deaf signers. While these studies did consider the comparability of the corpus, they were not focused on that aspect. Thanks to these studies, we may observe differences in sign performances among deaf signers, from crossed linguistics and computer science perspectives.

3 Computations on Sign Language Corpora

The computations in use for written data cannot be used directly for video SL corpora. Nowadays though, a way to study SL corpora is to annotate them. Annotations are mainly in written form, thus one might think of applying existing NLP methods to the resulting "texts". But would the conclusions be relevant enough? A bias is that annotations do not exactly represent SL utterances. Annotations can be made with glosses or complete translations but these written data cannot describe in an efficient way typical SL properties such as simultaneity, spatial organization, non-manual features, etc.

In our opinion, it would thus be difficult to apply the computations used on written comparable corpora (Fung, 2004; Morin, 2006; Deléger, 2008) or on parallel corpora to comparable or parallel SL corpora.

Some studies currently focus on graphical annotations, or use image processing to analyze video SL corpora (Bungeroth, 2008). It is a first step towards an analysis without any written text processing. Suitable tools to deal with this kind of annotations still have to be set up.

4 Promising Sign Language Corpora

4.1 Existing Corpora

The Dicta-Sign project already provides a quadrilingual corpus: the website contains four versions of the same presentation in four different sign languages. An analysis of this corpus would be interesting, because all SL videos were made from the English text. The British SL, and also the other texts in French, Greek, and German were obtained from the English written source. Then the corresponding SL videos in LSF, Greek SL, and German SL were translated from the texts in written French, Greek, and German. This corpus is therefore parallel, although probably noisy because of the double written-to-written then written-to-SL translation process. Comparing these videos would allow us to notice changes in the translations between SLs, using knowledge from the written-text translation field of research.

The corpus dealing with information in French railway stations is a bilingual parallel corpus. Other corpora are going to be designed and used in projects related to bus stations, airports, etc. Therefore we will have interesting parallel (French-LSF) and comparable (same topic) about transportation systems, to study.

4.2 Other Possible Corpora

The WebSourd Company's website [5] provides everyday news translations in LSF, displaying both the text that has been translated and the video in LSF. Each year, all videos are archived on a DVD. WebSourd is, as far as we know, the only company that provides everyday information in LSF. Collecting other sources for the same types of information would yield an interesting synchronous comparable corpus.

In SL we distinguish "translation" from "interpretation". Both could be performed either by hearing persons from vocal languages to SLs, and vice and versa, or by deaf persons from SLs to SLs. A translation is done with significant time taken for preparing the work. It looks more like a "written" form of language, thus such translations can create parallel corpora. Interpretation is done live, and often without any preparation of what is going to be interpreted. It is more like "oral" expression, with discourse corrections, repetitions, etc., thus it is likely to produce noisy corpora. SL interpretation corpora are available (e.g. every live interpretation on TV), but as far as we know they haven't yet been analyzed, although such study looks interesting.

There are in France[6] and in Great Britain[7] two TV programs presented in SL and made accessible with oral and written translations. These constitute a huge amount of parallel corpora (vocal language-sign language translations) that have not yet been used in any research field.

[5] http://www.websourd.org

[6] http://www.france5.fr/oeil-et-la-main/index-fr.php?page=accueil

[7] http://www.bbc.co.uk/blogs/seehear/

5 Conclusion

Until now very few parallel or comparable sign language corpora of SL have been built, and the few which exist were not studied from these points of view. Studying these parallel and comparable SL corpora for linguistics, computer science analysis, and for translation is therefore a new, yet to investigate area. What we should consider now is to set up a methodology to create those corpora with the aim to study them as what they are: parallel orcomparable. Moreover, we have to develop new tools, and adapt existing ones, that will fit this goal.

Reference

Roch-A. Bébian. 1825. *Mimographie, ou essai d'écriture mimique, propre à régulariser le langage des sourds-muets.* Paris. L. Colas eds.

Annelies Braffort, Christian Cuxac, Annick Choisier, Christophe Collet, Patrice Dalle, Ivani Fusellier, Rachid Gherbi, Guillemette Jausions, Gwenaelle Jirou, Fanch Lejeune, Boris Lenseigne, Nathalie Monteillard, Annie Risler, Marie-Anne Sallandre. 2001. *Projet LS-COLIN. Quel outil de notation pour quelle analyse de la LS ?* Colloque Recherches sur les langues des signes. Toulouse UTM eds. 71-86.

Hennie Brugman, Daan Broeder, and Gunter Senft. 2003. *Documentation of Languages and Archiving of Language Data at the Max Planck Insitute for Psycholinguistics in Nijmegen.* Ringvorlesung Bedrohte Sprachen. Bielefeld University, Germany.

Jan Bungeroth, Daniel Stein, Philippe Dreuw, Hermann Ney, Sara Morrissey, Andy Way and Lynette van Zijl. 2008. *The ATIS Sign Language Corpus.* 6th International Conference on Language Resources and Evaluation. Marrakech. Morocco.

Émilie Chételat-Pelé, Annelies Braffort. 2008. *Sign Language Corpus Annotation: Toward a New Methodology.* 6th International Conference on Language Resources and Evaluation. Marrakech. Morocco.

Christian Cuxac. 1996. *Fonctions et Structures de l'iconicité dans les langues des signes; analyse d'un idiolecte parisien de la Langues des Signes Française.* Doctoral Thesis, Paris V University, France.

Louise Deléger and Pierre Zweigenbaum. 2008. *Paraphrase acquisition from comparable medical corpora of specialized and lay texts.* AMIA. Annual Fall Symposium. Washington, DC. 146-150.

Eleni Efthimiou, Stavroula-Evita Fotinea, Christian Vogler, Thomas Hanke, John Glauert, Richard Bowden, Annelies Braffort, Christophe Collet, Petros Maragos, and Jérémie Segouat. 2009. *Sign Language Recognition, Generation and Modelling: A Research Effort with Applications in Deaf Communication.* 13th Internation Conference on Human-Computer Interaction. San Diego, CA. USA.

Pascale Fung, Percy Cheung. 2004. *Mining very-non-parallel corpora: Parallel sentence and lexicon extraction via bootstrapping and EM.* 12th Conference on Empirical Methods in Natural Language Processing. Barcelona. Spain. 57-63.

Brigitte Garcia, 2006. *The methodological, linguistic and semiological bases for the elaboration of a written form of LSF (French Sign Language).* 5th International Conference on Language Resources and Evaluation. Genoa. Italy.

Jean-Claude Martin, Jean-Paul Sansonnet, Annelies Braffort, and Cyril Verrecchia. 2009. *Informing the Design of Deictic Behaviors of a Web Agent with Spoken and Sign Language Video Data.* 8th International Gesture Workshop. Bielefeld, Germany.

Emmanuel Morin and Béatrice Daille. 2006. *Comparabilité de corpus et fouille terminologique multilingue.* Traitement Automatique des Langues. Vol 47. 113-136.

Carol Neidle. 2000. *SignStream(TM): A Database Tool for Research on Visual-Gestural Language.* American Sign Language Linguistic Research Project, Report No. 10. Boston University. USA.

Marie-Anne Sallandre. 2006. *Iconicity and Space in French Sign Language.* Space in languages: linguistic systems and cognitive categories. Collection Typological Studies in Language 66. John Benjamins. 239-255.

Jérémie Segouat, Annelies Braffort, and Émilie Martin. 2006. *Sign Language corpus analysis: Synchronisation of linguistic annotation and numerical data.* 5th International Conference on Language Resources and Evaluation - LREC, Genova, Italia.

Jérémie Segouat, Annelies Braffort, Laurence Bolot, Annick Choisier, Michael Filhol, and Cyril Verrecchia. 2008. *Building 3D French Sign Language lexicon.* 6th International Conference on Language Resources and Evaluation – LREC. Marrakech, Morocco.

Jérémie Segouat. 2009. *A Study of Sign Language Coarticulation.* Accessibility and Computing. SIGACCESS Newsletter. Issue 93. 31-38.

William C Stokoe, Dorothy C Casterline, and Carl G Croneberg. 1965. *A Dictionary of American Sign Language on Linguistic Principles.* Washington DC. Gallaudet College Press.

Author Index